BONUS
-MEAL PLANNING AND SHOPPING TIPS
-EXERCISE TIPS FOR OBESE PEOPLE

COOK BOOK
For Diabetics and High Cholesterol

OVER 150
Easy and tasty, Breakfast, Lunch, In-between Meal, Snacks, soups and Dinner Recipes for Obese and Diabetic People.

Emilia Chloe

Copyright

This cookbook is meant to help those who have diabetes, obesity, or other associated conditions, but it is not meant to take the place of medical advice. Please get medical counsel before making any dietary modifications.

Table of Contents

15. Cucumber Salad:

16. Lentil Burgers:

17. Zucchini Noodles:

18. Butternut Squash Soup:

19. Hummus:

20. Baked Apples:

21. Sweet Potato Hash:

22. Baked Falafel:

23. Turkey Burgers:

24. Green Bean Salad:

25. Cauliflower Rice:

26. Baked Fish:

27. Eggplant Parmesan:

2. Lunch Recipes

1. Zucchini Noodles with Turkey Meatballs:

2. Roasted Cauliflower Rice Bowl:

3. Broccoli and Quinoa Salad:

4. Turkey and Sweet Potato Hash:

5. Turkey Lettuce Wraps:

6. Tomato and Spinach Salad:

7. Baked Salmon with Asparagus:

8. Zucchini Fritters:

9. Egg Salad with Avocado:

10. Cucumber and Tomato Salad:

11. Grilled Chicken and Vegetables:

12. Quinoa Bowl with Roasted Veggies:

13. Overnight Oats:

14. Turkey Burgers with Sweet Potato Fries:

15. Turkey and Spinach Lasagna:

16. Roasted Brussels Sprouts and Sweet Potatoes:

17. Stuffed Peppers:

18. Baked Cod with Broccoli:

19. Lentil Soup:

20. Quinoa Stuffed Acorn Squash:

21. Baked Chicken with Sweet Potato:

22. Turkey and Zucchini Meatballs:

23. Avocado and Egg Salad:

24. Broccoli and Quinoa Bowl:

25. Roasted Veggies and Brown Rice:

26. Baked Salmon with Asparagus:

27. Grilled Chicken and Veggies:

28. Lentil and Quinoa Salad:

29. Baked Tofu with Broccoli:

30. Egg and Avocado Wrap:

3. Dinner Recipes

1. Baked Salmon with Asparagus

2. Roasted Chicken Breast with Broccoli

3. Grilled Turkey and Vegetable Stir-Fry

4. Quinoa Salad with Roasted Vegetables

5. Slow Cooker Vegetable Soup

6. Salmon and Brown Rice Bowl

7. Grilled Shrimp with Zucchini and Squash

8. Chickpea and Spinach Curry

9. Greek Salad with Feta and Olives

10. Lentil and Kale Stew

11. Grilled Vegetable and Tofu Kabobs

12. Turkey and Quinoa Stuffed Peppers

13. Roasted Vegetable and Barley Bowl

14. Baked Tilapia with Tomatoes and Herbs

15. Grilled Vegetable and Hummus Wraps

16. Spaghetti Squash with Turkey Meatballs

17. Stuffed Mushroom Caps

18. Grilled Salmon and Vegetable Kabobs

19. Zucchini Noodles with Pesto

20. Baked Sweet Potatoes with Greek Yogurt and Berries

4. Snack Recipes

1. Celery and Hummus:

2. Baked Kale Chips:

3. Greek Yogurt Parfait:

4. Smoothie Bowl:

5. Bean Burrito:

6. Avocado Toast:

7. Quinoa Bowl:

8. Apple Slices with Peanut Butter:

9. Zucchini Fries:

10. Overnight Oats:

11. Cucumber Tomato Salad:

12. Baked Sweet Potato Fries:

13. Chocolate Banana Bites:

14. Chickpea Salad:

15. Edamame:

16. Popcorn:

17. Carrot Sticks and Hummus:

18. Fruit Salad:

19. Trail Mix:

20. Egg Salad:

5. VEGETABLE OPTIONS

1. Lentil and Kale Soup:

2. Broccoli and Mushroom Stir-Fry:

3. Cauliflower Curry:

4. Zucchini and Tomato Bake:

5. Eggplant and Spinach Salad:

6. Roasted Cabbage:

7. Lentil and Carrot Stew:

8. Roasted Sweet Potato and Asparagus:

9. Quinoa and Vegetable Bowl:

10. Vegetable Lasagna:

11. Chickpea Curry:

12. Roasted Brussels Sprouts:

13. Broccoli and Cauliflower Salad:

14. Ratatouille:

15. Butternut Squash Soup:

16. Stuffed Peppers:

17. Lentil and Spinach Salad:

18. Baked Eggplant Parmesan:

19. Roasted Vegetable Bowl:

20. Cabbage and Carrot Slaw:

C. Tips for Eating Healthy

Meal Planning and Shopping Tips

Meal prep ideas for busy weeks

Exercise Suggestions For Obese People

Conclusion

Cookbook

For

Diabetes and

High Cholesterol

Preface.

Obesity and diabetes are prevalent health issues in today's society. As a result, many people are looking for methods to manage their weight while still enjoying in delectable foods. This cookbook provides a range of meals that are healthy for diabetes and overweight people without sacrificing taste or enjoyment.

This cookbook has a wide variety of recipes that employ healthy ingredients and cooking methods to create delicious and fulfilling meals. All of the recipes were specifically developed to be high in fiber, low in sugar, and low in fat. Many of the recipes are also low in calories, making them ideal for anyone trying to reduce weight or improve their health.

This cookbook is meant to help you discover new and fascinating ways to manage your weight while still enjoying in delicious food. Everybody may find something they like, from simple snacks to hearty feasts. We've also included helpful tips on how to maximize the recipes and create delicious, nutritious meals you can cook every day.

This cookbook is meant to be a tool for you, one that will help you lead a healthy lifestyle while enjoying nourishing and delicious meals. Happy eating!

Introduction.

A. DIABETES AND OBESITY DEFINED

There there was a woman named Mary who struggled with her weight and her health. After being diagnosed with diabetes and obesity, she had been trying to regulate her health and weight. No matter how many diets and exercise plans she tried, nothing seemed to work. She was frustrated and felt powerless. Then, one day, Mary stumbled onto a cookbook made exclusively for fat and diabetic people. She was ecstatic! For the first time in a long time, she was hopeful that something might finally function. She decided to evaluate the cookbook. The booklet was packed with delicious, healthy recipes created especially for diabetes and obese people. With each dish, Mary was able to learn more about the nutritional benefits of the ingredients and how to prepare them. She was able to maintain a healthy diet and get the required amount of calories from each meal.

The cookbook also included tips for living a healthy lifestyle, which was quite helpful. Mary gained knowledge on how to have a healthy lifestyle and choose nutritious foods. She had the ability to make little lifestyle changes that had a big effect on her overall health. Mary found the results to be astounding. After following the meal plans and lifestyle advice in the cookbook, she was able to manage her diabetes and shed some weight. Since she was now living a better, happier life, she was grateful to the cookbook for making it all possible.

Mary's story is an excellent example of how important having the ideal cookbook can be. With the right recipes and lifestyle advice, anybody who suffers with obesity and diabetes may make the necessary changes to improve their health and quality of life.

Greetings from the delicious and nutritious cooking for diabetes globe! You might enjoy the best of both worlds with the aid of this cookbook: delectable recipes that are also nutritious. This cookbook includes a wide range of recipes that may be included into any diabetic's diet plan, from light and refreshing salads to hearty and delicious main dishes. Since all of the meals are prepared using wholesome and fresh ingredients, you can be sure that you are getting the best nutrition available. By utilizing this cookbook, we intend to improve the enjoyment, flavor, and nutritional value of meals. Enjoy!

OBESITY

An individual is deemed obese if their BMI is 30 or more, which is recognized as a clinically relevant level of obesity.

An individual who has an unusually high amount of body fat is said to have obesity. The common definition is having a body mass index (BMI) of 30 or above. Obesity raises the risk factors for heart disease, type 2 diabetes, and stroke. Treatment plans may include dietary and activity modifications, such as adopting a balanced diet.

DIABETES

Diabetes is a chronic medical condition in which the body is unable to produce or use the hormone insulin, which helps regulate blood sugar (glucose) levels.

Lack of insulin stops glucose from entering the cells, resulting in blood glucose levels rising and a host of health problems.

Diabetes sufferers should eat properly since it reduces their risk of complications and aids in blood sugar control. Low in salt and saturated fat, a balanced diet rich in fresh fruits, vegetables, and whole grains may help regulate blood sugar levels and reduce the risk of complications from diabetes. Exercise is also essential for managing diabetes and improving overall health.

B. BENEFITS OF HEALTHY EATING FOR DIABETIC AND OBESE PEOPLE

Over one-third of Americans are obese, and 10.5% of people in the US have diabetes. For controlling chronic illnesses and improving overall health, a nutritious diet is essential. Eating a balanced diet may help people with diabetes and obesity reduce their risk of serious health problems including heart disease, stroke, type 2 diabetes, and some types of cancer.

Healthy diet may help people with diabetes and obesity in a number of ways. In addition to lowering the risk of diabetic consequences including nerve damage, heart disease, and kidney failure, a balanced diet may also assist diabetics regulate their blood sugar levels. A balanced diet may help diabetics lose weight, which will improve their overall health and reduce their risk of developing type 2 diabetes.

A balanced diet may help obese people lose weight and reduce their risk of serious health problems. By consuming a balanced diet full of nutrient-dense foods and low in calories, people may reduce their risk of obesity-related health problems including heart disease, stroke, type 2 diabetes, and some types of cancer. A healthy diet may help prevent heart disease in addition to decreasing cholesterol levels.

A healthy diet may also improve a person's quality of life by increasing their energy and mood. A balanced diet that is high in fiber, fruits, vegetables, and whole grains and low in saturated, trans, and cholesterol may help people feel fuller for longer, have fewer cravings, and better regulate their appetite. A balanced diet may help people with diabetes and obesity by providing them with the essential vitamins, minerals, and other nutrients they need for good health.

Overall, eating properly may help you maintain a healthy weight and manage diabetes and obesity. Eating a balanced diet full of nutrient-dense foods and low in calories may help people with diabetes and obesity improve their quality of life and reduce their risk of serious health problems.

PART 1:

Basics of Healthy Eating for Obese and Diabetic People

1. Understanding Nutrition and Macronutrients

Nutrition affects both a healthy weight and excellent health. It's especially important to understand nutrition and macronutrients when it comes to obesity and diabetes.

The first step in managing an obese person's or diabetic person's condition is to understand how nutrition impacts health. Choosing the right things to eat and cutting down on sugar, processed meals, and other hazardous substances will help you control your weight and enhance your overall health.

Carbs, proteins, and lipids are the three macronutrients that are most important for someone who is overweight and diabetic. Since they are the body's main source of energy, carbohydrates should make up the majority of a person's diet. Picking complex carbohydrates over simple ones, like white bread, white rice, and sugary snacks, is crucial. These consist of fruits, vegetables, whole grains, and legumes. These complex carbohydrates provide the body essential vitamins and minerals as well as fiber, which may help regulate blood sugar levels and reduce cravings.

Protein is a crucial macronutrient for growing and repairing muscle and other tissues. The diet should include lean proteins from a variety of sources, including lean meats, fish, eggs, nuts, and seeds.

Fats not only provide a large amount of energy but also have the potential to reduce cravings. However, it's critical to choose monounsaturated and polyunsaturated fats over saturated and trans fats, which are included in processed meals, fried foods, and margarine. These fats may be found in nuts, seeds, olive oil, and avocados.

For those with diabetes or obesity, understanding how nutrition and macronutrients impact their health is crucial. A balanced diet with a variety of nutrient-dense proteins, carbohydrates, and fats may help control blood sugar levels, manage cravings, and promote weight reduction. This could improve people's overall health and quality of life.

2. Understanding Nutrition and Micro Nutrients.

Nutrition is essential for maintaining health and preventing disease. For individuals with diabetes or obesity to preserve their health, they must have a thorough understanding of diet and micronutrients.

Obesity is associated with a number of health risks, including heart disease, stroke, type 2 diabetes, and several types of cancer. A balanced diet and regular exercise are essential components of any program for weight loss success. A balanced diet that excludes hazardous foods like saturated fat, trans fat, and added sugars is advocated. This diet should include foods from all of the major food groups. Eating in smaller portions, abstaining from or reducing the use of sugary drinks, and limiting processed and fast food are further weight-management techniques.

Micronutrients are essential vitamins and minerals that the body needs in trace amounts to function properly. A broad variety of foods, including dairy products, nuts, cereals, fruits, vegetables, meat, and fish, may contain them. Calcium, magnesium, iron, vitamin C, vitamin A, and vitamin C are examples of micronutrients. Eating a variety of meals rich in micronutrients may help you maintain a healthy weight and satisfy your nutritional needs.

Diet is important for everyone, but especially for those with diabetes. Eating a balanced diet is necessary for keeping blood sugar under control and preventing problems. Eating meals low in carbohydrates, including fruits and vegetables, may help keep blood sugar levels constant. Additionally, eating complex carbohydrates, lean proteins, and healthy fats during meals and snacks is encouraged. Smaller, frequent meals may also help to keep blood sugar levels constant.

Furthermore, those who have diabetes need to be mindful of their micronutrient intake. Micronutrients including chromium, zinc, and magnesium have been demonstrated to help regulate blood sugar levels. Consuming foods high in these micronutrients, such as legumes, whole grains, nuts, and seeds, aids in maintaining normal blood sugar levels.

A comprehensive understanding of nutrition and micronutrients is necessary for maintaining good health and preventing sickness, especially for those who are obese or have diabetes. Eating a balanced diet rich in micronutrients and low in unhealthy fats and added sugars may help people maintain a healthy weight and manage their blood sugar levels.

3. Choosing Healthy Foods for Diabetes and Obesity.

One of the most important considerations for dieting and health is choosing healthy meals for diabetes and obese people. Eating the right foods is important for overall health and wellbeing and may help with blood sugar and weight management.

A focus should be placed on eating nutrient-dense meals that are minimal in calories and sugar for those who are overweight or have diabetes. A balanced diet with plenty of fresh fruits and vegetables is crucial for these individuals. Maintaining a healthy weight and blood sugar levels depends on consuming the essential vitamins, minerals, and other substances that may be found in fruits and vegetables.

In addition to fresh fruits and vegetables, a healthy diet for obese and diabetic people should also include whole grains, lentils, and lean meats. Whole grains include necessary fiber and complex carbs that may help control blood sugar levels. Legumes are an excellent source of protein, which supports the development and maintenance of muscles. Lean proteins, such those found in fish, poultry, and eggs, are good for managing weight.

It's important to limit processed meals, refined carbs, and unhealthy fats like trans-fats while aiming to eat healthily. These foods are widely known for causing weight gain, high blood sugar levels, and other health problems. Instead, concentrate on consuming natural, fresh foods low in sugar and saturated fats.

Finally, those with diabetes or obesity should be sure to get adequate water and exercise often. Getting enough water may help remove toxins and speed up metabolism. For one to be physically fit and at a healthy weight, exercise is essential. Try to get in at least 30 minutes of physical activity each day.

Obese and diabetic people may control their health and fitness by following these suggestions and placing a focus on eating nutrient-dense, fresh meals. Good eating may help you maintain a healthy weight, manage your blood sugar levels, and improve your overall health.

4. Preparing Healthy Meals for Diabetics and Obese People

A healthy diet is necessary for both overweight and diabetic people. Even if it may be difficult to prepare meals that meet the nutritional demands of both groups, it is possible to create delicious and healthy dishes that may improve health and wellbeing.

When it comes to diabetes, concentrating on meals that are high in fiber and low in carbohydrates may help to normalize blood sugar levels. Fresh vegetables, lean meats, and whole grains may be quite beneficial in diabetic meals. It's also important to limit processed and sugary foods since they might cause blood sugar spikes and unhealthy weight gain.

For obese people, meals should include lean proteins, healthy fats, and complex carbohydrates. Since fresh fruit includes essential vitamins and minerals, eating a lot of it has additional benefits. It's critical to limit saturated and trans fats, as well as processed and sugary foods.

When cooking meals, it is essential to plan ahead. You can maximize your time in the kitchen and make sure you have the right ingredients on hand by preparing meals in advance. It is important to make sure that meals are balanced and nutritious since this will help to give the energy and nutrients needed to maintain health and fitness.

By making wholesome meals for diabetics and obese people, you may improve their health and wellbeing. With a little planning and creativity, it is possible to create delicious, satisfying meals that are also beneficial for your health.

5. Understanding Nutrition and Meal Serving Sizes.

For diabetics and obese people, it's critical to understand nutrition and meal portion proportions. It's important to understand which meals to eat, when to eat them, and how much of each thing to eat. With the help of the right meal combinations and portion sizes, it is possible to maintain a healthy weight, control blood sugar levels, reduce the risk of developing diabetes, and address other health issues.

For those with diabetes and obesity, it's crucial to concentrate on a balanced diet that's high in fiber, vitamins, minerals, and other critical nutrients while being low in saturated fat, trans fat, cholesterol, salt, and added sweets. Additionally, it's important to keep an eye on portion sizes and eat a variety of wholesome meals from each food group.

DIABETES

People with diabetes are advised by the American Diabetes Association (ADA) to focus on eating a balanced diet that is high in fiber, vitamins, minerals, and other necessary nutrients while being low in saturated fat, trans fat, cholesterol, salt, and added sugars. The ADA also suggests that people with diabetes control their portion sizes and eat a variety of wholesome meals from each food group.

The ADA urges people with diabetes to utilize the plate approach for determining portion sizes. A person should fill half of their plate with non-starchy vegetables, one-fourth of it with lean protein, and one-fourth of it with grains or starchy vegetables, according to the plate method. The ADA also suggests that diabetics add a serving of fruit, dairy, or good fats in their diet.

OBESITY

Obese people are advised to focus on eating a balanced diet that is high in fiber, vitamins, minerals, and other necessary nutrients and low in calories, saturated fat, trans fat, cholesterol, salt, and added sweets by the National Institute of Diabetes and Digestive and Kidney Diseases (NIDDK). The NIDDK also suggests that obese people watch their portion sizes and eat a variety of wholesome meals from each food group.

Obese people are advised by the NIDDK to focus on eating smaller meals at more regular intervals throughout the day. Obese individuals should also limit their intake of processed and high-calorie meals and focus on eating a range of nutritious foods from each dietary group. The NIDDK also suggests that obese people add a serving of fruit, dairy, or healthy fats with their meal.

It is critical for people with diabetes and obesity to comprehend nutrition and meal portion sizes in order to maintain a healthy weight and reduce their chance of developing diabetes and other health issues. Maintaining healthy blood sugar levels and a healthy weight may be made easier by knowing the right meal combinations and serving sizes.

Part 2:

Recipes for Obese and Diabetic People

Welcome to this collection of dishes for diabetic and chubby folks! Controlling diabetes and obesity requires maintaining a healthy, balanced diet. For this reason, meals should be prepared to be both filling and delectable. For breakfast, lunch, and dinner, you may find low-sugar, low-fat, high-fiber, and protein-rich foods here. These dishes may help you attain and maintain a healthy weight and blood sugar levels since they are sure to provide the perfect balance of nutrition and flavor. Enjoy!

Disclaimer: Some of the images that are added to each recipe are not direct representations of how the recipes appear; instead, they suggest several ways to prepare meals, show the ingredients, or are exact replicas of the recipe.

1.

Breakfast Recipes

1. Roasted Broccoli and Cauliflower

Ingredients:

-1 head of broccoli, cut into florets

-1 head of cauliflower, cut into florets

-2 tablespoons olive oil

-1 teaspoon garlic powder

-1 teaspoon onion powder

-1/2 teaspoon salt

-1/4 teaspoon black pepper

Instructions:

1. Preheat the oven to 400 degrees F.

2. In a large bowl, combine the broccoli and cauliflower florets.

3. Drizzle the olive oil over the vegetables and toss to coat.

4. Sprinkle the garlic powder, onion powder, salt and pepper over the vegetables and toss to coat.

5. Place the vegetables on a baking sheet and spread in an even layer.

6. Roast for 25-30 minutes, stirring halfway through, until the vegetables are tender and beginning to brown.

7. Serve warm. Enjoy!

2. Grilled Salmon

Ingredients

-Salmon fillet (4-6 ounces per person)

-Olive oil

-Salt and pepper

-Optional: Fresh herbs, garlic, lemon juice

Instructions

1. Preheat your grill to medium heat.

2. Rinse the salmon fillet and pat dry with a paper towel.

3. Rub the salmon with olive oil and season with salt and pepper.

4. Place the salmon on the preheated grill and cook for 4-6 minutes per side, depending on the thickness of the fillet.

5. Optional: Add fresh herbs, garlic, and lemon juice to the salmon while it's cooking.

6. Remove the salmon from the grill and serve. Enjoy!

3. Quinoa and Veggie Stir-Fry

Ingredients:

-2 tablespoons of olive oil

-1 cup of quinoa

-2 cloves of garlic, minced

-1 red bell pepper, diced

-1/2 cup of carrots, diced

-1/2 cup of broccoli, chopped

-1/4 cup of red onion, diced

-1/4 cup of mushrooms, diced

-1/4 cup of frozen peas

-Salt and pepper, to taste

Instructions:

1. Heat the olive oil in a large skillet over medium-high heat.

2. Add the quinoa and cook, stirring frequently, for 4-5 minutes, or until it is lightly toasted.

3. Add the garlic, bell pepper, carrots, broccoli, onion, and mushrooms and continue to cook, stirring often, for 3-4 minutes, or until the vegetables are slightly softened.

4. Add the peas and season with salt and pepper.

5. Cover the skillet and reduce the heat to medium-low. Cook for 10-12 minutes, or until the quinoa is cooked through and the vegetables are tender.

6. Serve the quinoa and veggie stir-fry warm. Enjoy

4. Greek Yogurt Parfait:

Layer Greek yogurt, fresh berries, and a sprinkle of nut or seed of your choice.

Ingredients:

-1 cup plain Greek yogurt

-1/4 cup granola

-1/4 cup blueberries

-1/4 cup strawberries

-1/4 cup blackberries

Step by Step Method:

1. In a bowl, add 1 cup of Greek yogurt and mix well.

2. Place the yogurt in a parfait glass.

3. Sprinkle 1/4 cup of granola over the yogurt.

4. Place 1/4 cup of blueberries, strawberries, and blackberries over the granola.

5. Serve and enjoy!

5. Baked Tilapia with Spinach:

Place a piece of tilapia in a baking dish with a drizzle of olive oil, garlic, and lemon juice. Top with a handful of fresh spinach leaves.

Ingredients:

-4 tilapia fillets

-1 tablespoon olive oil

-1 teaspoon garlic powder

-1/4 teaspoon salt

-1/4 teaspoon ground black pepper

-2 cups fresh spinach

-1/4 cup grated Parmesan cheese

Steps:

1. Preheat oven to 350 degrees F.

2. Place tilapia fillets in a greased baking dish.

3. Drizzle olive oil over the fillets and sprinkle with garlic powder, salt, and pepper.

4. Top with fresh spinach and sprinkle Parmesan cheese on top.

5. Bake in preheated oven for 15-20 minutes, or until fish is cooked through and flakes easily with a fork.

6. Serve and enjoy!

6. Chickpea Curry:

Cook chickpeas in a pot with curry powder, onion, garlic, and low-sodium vegetable broth.

Ingredients:

-1 can of chickpeas (drained and rinsed)

-1 onion (chopped)

-2 cloves of garlic (minced)

-1 teaspoon of ground cumin

-1 teaspoon of ground coriander

-1 teaspoon of garam masala

-1 teaspoon of chili powder

-1/2 teaspoon of turmeric

-1 can of diced tomatoes

-1/2 cup of water

-1/4 cup of coconut milk

-Salt and pepper to taste

Method:

1. Heat a large pot over medium-high heat and add the chopped onion. Cook until the onion is softened and lightly browned (about 5 minutes).

2. Add the minced garlic and all of the spices. Stir and cook for another minute or so.

3. Add the chickpeas, diced tomatoes, water, and coconut milk. Bring the mixture to a boil.

4. Reduce the heat to low and simmer for 20 minutes, stirring occasionally.

5. Taste and adjust the seasonings as needed. Serve with rice or naan. Enjoy!

7. Lentil Soup:

Cook lentils in a pot with low-sodium vegetable broth, onion, garlic, and seasonings of your choice.

Ingredients:

- 1 cup of lentils
- 2 tablespoons of olive oil
- 1 onion, chopped
- 2 cloves of garlic, minced
- 3 carrots, chopped
- 2 stalks of celery, chopped
- 1 teaspoon of ground cumin
- 4 cups of vegetable broth
- Salt and pepper to taste

Instructions:

1. Heat the olive oil in a large pot over medium heat.

2. Add the onion, garlic, carrots, and celery and sauté until the vegetables are softened, about 5 minutes.

3. Stir in the cumin and cook for another minute.

4. Add the lentils and vegetable broth and bring to a boil.

5. Reduce the heat and simmer for 20-25 minutes, or until the lentils are tender.

6. Season with salt and pepper to taste.

7. Serve warm. Enjoy!

8. Baked Sweet Potato Fries:

Slice sweet potatoes into fry shapes and toss in a bowl with a small amount of olive oil and seasoning. Place on a baking sheet and bake in the oven.

Ingredients:

- 2 sweet potatoes, peeled and cut into long, thin fry shapes
- 2 tablespoons of olive oil
- 1 teaspoon of garlic powder
- 1/2 teaspoon of paprika
- 1/2 teaspoon of onion powder
- 1/2 teaspoon of salt

Instructions:

1. Preheat oven to 425°F.
2. Peel and cut sweet potatoes into thin fry shapes.
3. Place sweet potato fries in a large bowl and add olive oil, garlic powder, paprika, onion powder, and salt.
4. Toss to coat sweet potato fries with the mixture.
5. Line a baking sheet with parchment paper and spread out the fries onto the baking sheet.
6. Bake for 10 minutes, then flip the fries over and bake for an additional 10 minutes.
7. Remove from oven and serve. Enjoy!

9. Egg White Omelet:

Whisk together egg whites and seasonings of your choice. Cook in a non-stick pan with a small amount of olive oil or cooking spray.

Ingredients:

-2 eggs

-2 tablespoons of milk

-Salt and pepper

-1 tablespoon of butter

-Chopped vegetables (optional)

Steps:

1. Crack the eggs into a bowl and separate the yolks from the whites.
2. Whisk the egg whites until they are fluffy.

3. Add the milk, salt, and pepper to the egg whites and whisk until combined.
4. Heat a non-stick skillet over medium heat and add the butter.

5. Once the butter is melted, pour in the egg whites and spread them out evenly.
6. If desired, add chopped vegetables to the top of the egg whites.

7. Cook the egg whites until they are golden brown, about 2-3 minutes.
8. Carefully flip the omelet over and cook for an additional 1-2 minutes.

9. Serve the egg white omelet with desired toppings. Enjoy!

10. Avocado Toast:

Toast whole-grain bread and top with mashed avocado, a sprinkle of salt, and lemon juice.

Ingredients:

- 2 slices of whole-grain bread
- 1/2 of an avocado
- 2 teaspoons of olive oil
- 2 teaspoons of lime juice
- Salt and pepper to taste
- Optional toppings (such as cherry tomatoes, feta cheese, and/or smoked salmon)

Instructions:

1. Preheat the oven to 350 degrees Fahrenheit.
2. Toast the bread in the preheated oven for 5-7 minutes, or until lightly golden.
3. Meanwhile, mash the avocado in a bowl.
4. Add the olive oil and lime juice to the mashed avocado and mix until combined.
5. Spread the avocado mixture onto the toasted bread slices.
6. Sprinkle with salt and pepper to taste.
7. Add desired toppings and serve immediately.

11. Kale and Berry Smoothie:

Blend together a handful of kale, a handful of frozen berries, and a cup of unsweetened almond milk

Ingredients:

- 1 cup kale leaves (chopped)
- ½ cup blueberries
- ½ cup raspberries
- 1 banana
- ½ cup almond milk
- ½ cup orange juice
- 2 tablespoons honey
- 2 tablespoons chia seeds

Step by Step Method:

1. Place the chopped kale leaves in a blender.

2. Add blueberries, raspberries and banana to the blender.

3. Pour the almond milk, orange juice, honey and chia seeds into the blender.

4. Blend all the ingredients until they are smooth.

5. Pour the smoothie into a glass and enjoy!.

12. Baked Chicken Breast:

Bake a chicken breast in the oven with a small amount of olive oil, garlic, and lemon juice.

Ingredients:

- 4 boneless, skinless chicken breasts
- 2 tablespoons olive oil
- 1 teaspoon garlic powder
- 1 teaspoon onion powder
- 1 teaspoon paprika
- 1 teaspoon dried oregano
- Salt and pepper, to taste

Steps:

1. Preheat oven to 375°F.
2. Line a baking sheet with parchment paper.
3. Place chicken breasts on the prepared baking sheet.
4. Drizzle olive oil over the chicken breasts and use your hands to rub it into the chicken.
5. Sprinkle garlic powder, onion powder, paprika, oregano, salt and pepper over the chicken breasts.
6. Bake in preheated oven for 25-30 minutes, or until chicken is cooked through.
7. Serve with your favorite side dishes. Enjoy!

13. Overnight Oats:

Combine rolled oats, chia seeds, unsweetened almond milk, and your favorite spices. Let sit in the fridge overnight.

Ingredients:

- 1/2 cup rolled oats
- 1/2 cup milk of your choice
- 1/2 cup plain yogurt
- 1 tablespoon chia seeds
- 1 tablespoon honey or maple syrup
- 1/2 teaspoon ground cinnamon
- 1/4 teaspoon vanilla extract
- Optional toppings of your choice

Steps:

1. In a medium bowl, mix together the oats, milk, yogurt, chia seeds, honey or maple syrup, cinnamon, and vanilla extract until combined.

2. Cover the bowl with plastic wrap or a lid and place it in the refrigerator overnight.

3. In the morning, remove the bowl from the refrigerator and stir the mixture.

4. Serve the oats in a bowl with your desired toppings. Enjoy!

14. Baked Squash:

Cut a squash in half, drizzle with olive oil, garlic, and spices, and bake in the oven.

Ingredients:

-1 squash (any variety)
-1 tablespoon olive oil
-Salt and pepper to taste

Instructions:

1. Preheat oven to 400°F.
2. Cut squash in half lengthwise and remove the seeds.
3. Place squash halves on a baking sheet lined with parchment paper or a silicone baking mat.
4. Drizzle the cut sides of the squash with the olive oil, salt and pepper.
5. Bake for 25-30 minutes, or until the squash is tender.
6. Serve hot. Enjoy!

15. Cucumber Salad:

Slice cucumbers into thin slices and top with a small amount of olive oil, vinegar, garlic, and herbs.

Ingredients:

- 2 cucumbers, thinly sliced
- 2 tablespoons white vinegar
- 2 tablespoons olive oil
- 1 teaspoon sugar
- 1 teaspoon salt
- 1/2 teaspoon black pepper
- 2 tablespoons fresh dill, chopped
- 2 tablespoons red onion, chopped

Instructions:

1. Slice the cucumbers into thin slices and place them in a large bowl.
2. In a separate bowl, mix together the vinegar, olive oil, sugar, salt, and pepper.
3. Pour the dressing over the cucumbers and mix until all of the cucumbers are evenly coated.
4. Add the dill and red onion and mix to combine.
5. Serve chilled or at room temperature. Enjoy!

16. Lentil Burgers:

Combine cooked lentils, oats, and seasonings in a food processor and form into patties. Bake or grill in a pan with a small amount of olive oil.

Ingredients:

-1 cup brown or green lentils

-1/2 cup cooked quinoa

-1/2 cup chopped onion

-1/2 cup chopped bell pepper

-1/2 cup chopped mushrooms

-1/4 cup rolled oats

-1/4 cup cooked brown rice

-1 teaspoon garlic powder

-1 teaspoon dried oregano

-1 teaspoon smoked paprika

-1 teaspoon ground cumin

-1/2 teaspoon sea salt

-1/4 teaspoon black pepper

-1/4 cup olive oil

Step by Step Method:

1. Preheat your oven to 375°F (190°C).

2. Rinse the lentils and place them in a medium saucepan. Cover with 2 inches of water and bring to a boil. Reduce the heat to a simmer and cook for 15 minutes or until the lentils are tender. Drain the lentils and set aside.

3. In a large bowl, combine the cooked lentils, quinoa, onion, bell pepper, mushrooms, oats, brown rice, garlic powder, oregano, smoked paprika, cumin, sea salt, and black pepper. Mix until everything is well combined.

4. Using a spoon or your hands, form the mixture into 8 patties.

5. Heat the olive oil in a large skillet over medium-high heat. Add the patties to the skillet and cook for 5 minutes or until golden brown. Flip the patties and cook for an additional 3 minutes.

6. Transfer the patties to a parchment-lined baking sheet and bake for 15 minutes or until cooked through.

7. Serve the Lentil Burgers with your favorite toppings and sides. Enjoy!

17. Zucchini Noodles:

Use a spiralizer to create "noodles" out of zucchini. Saute in a pan with a small amount of olive oil and garlic.

Ingredients

-3 medium zucchinis
-1 tablespoon olive oil
-Salt and pepper
-Optional toppings (parmesan cheese, garlic powder, red pepper flakes, etc.)

Instructions

1. Using a spiralizer or julienne peeler, cut the zucchini into noodles.
2. Heat the olive oil in a large skillet over medium heat.
3. Add the zucchini noodles to the skillet and season with salt and pepper.
4. Cook for about 5 minutes, stirring occasionally, until the noodles are tender.
5. Serve with desired toppings and enjoy

18. Butternut Squash Soup:

Combine cubed butternut squash, onion, garlic, and seasonings in a pot with low-sodium vegetable broth. Simmer until squash is tender.

Ingredients:
-1 butternut squash (peeled, seeded, and diced)
-1 onion (chopped)
-2 tablespoons of olive oil
-2 cloves of garlic (minced)
-4 cups of vegetable broth
-1 teaspoon of dried thyme
-1 teaspoon of dried sage
-Salt and pepper to taste

Instructions:
1. Preheat oven to 400 degrees Fahrenheit.
2. Place the diced butternut squash on a baking sheet and drizzle with olive oil. Roast for about 20 minutes, or until the squash is tender.
3. Heat olive oil in a large pot over medium heat.
4. Add the onion and garlic and sauté until softened, about 5 minutes.
5. Add the roasted butternut squash, vegetable broth, thyme, and sage. Bring to a simmer and cook for 10 minutes.
6. Carefully transfer the soup to a blender or food processor and blend until smooth.
7. Return the soup to the pot and season with salt and pepper to taste.
8. Simmer for an additional 10 minutes.
9. Serve warm. Enjoy!

19. Hummus:

Blend together chickpeas, tahini, garlic, and lemon juice. Serve with raw vegetables.

Ingredients:

-1 can chickpeas, drained and rinsed
-3 tablespoons tahini
-2 cloves garlic, minced
-2 tablespoons olive oil
-2 tablespoons lemon juice
-1/2 teaspoon cumin
-Salt and pepper to taste

Instructions:

1. Place the drained and rinsed chickpeas, tahini, garlic, olive oil, lemon juice, cumin, salt and pepper into a food processor or blender.
2. Blend the ingredients until the hummus is creamy and smooth.
3. Taste and adjust seasonings as needed.
4. Serve the hummus with warm pita bread or vegetables for dipping. Enjoy!

20. Baked Apples:

Core and slice apples and place on a baking sheet. Drizzle with a small amount of maple syrup, cinnamon, and nutmeg. Bake in the oven.

Ingredients:

- 4 apples

- 2 tablespoons butter

- 2 tablespoons brown sugar

- 1 teaspoon ground cinnamon

- ½ teaspoon nutmeg

- 1/4 cup of water

Step by Step Method:

1. Preheat oven to 375 degrees F (190 degrees C).

2. Core the apples and place them in a baking dish.

3. In a small bowl, mix together the butter, brown sugar, cinnamon, and nutmeg.

4. Stuff the apples with the mixture.

5. Pour the water into the bottom of the baking dish.

6. Bake for 30 minutes, or until the apples are tender.

7. Serve warm. Enjoy!

21. Sweet Potato Hash:

Slice sweet potatoes into cubes and sauté in a pan with a small amount of olive oil, onions, and garlic.

Ingredients:

- 2 sweet potatoes, diced
- 1 onion, diced
- 2 tablespoons olive oil
- Salt and pepper, to taste

Steps:

1. Preheat a large skillet over medium-high heat.
2. Add the olive oil to the skillet, then add the diced sweet potatoes and onion.
3. Cook, stirring occasionally, until the potatoes are golden brown and cooked through, about 10-15 minutes.
4. Add salt and pepper to taste.
5. Serve warm.

22. Baked Falafel:

Combine canned chickpeas, onions, garlic, and spices in a food processor and form into patties. Bake in the oven.

Ingredients:

-2 cups of cooked chickpeas

-1/2 cup chopped onion

-1/4 cup minced parsley

-1/4 cup minced cilantro

-2 cloves garlic, minced

-2 tablespoons ground cumin

-1 teaspoon ground coriander

-1 teaspoon baking powder

-1/2 teaspoon sea salt

-1/4 teaspoon black pepper

-3 tablespoons olive oil

Instructions:

1. Preheat oven to 400 degrees F.
2. Place chickpeas into a food processor and pulse until coarsely chopped.
3. Transfer the chickpeas to a large bowl and add the onion, parsley, cilantro, garlic, cumin, coriander, baking powder, salt, and pepper.
4. Mix everything together until combined.
5. Form the mixture into 2-inch balls and place on a greased baking sheet.
6. Drizzle the falafel balls with olive oil.
7. Bake for 20 minutes, flipping the falafel balls halfway through.
8. Serve warm with your favorite dips and accompaniments. Enjoy!

23. Turkey Burgers:

Combine ground turkey, oats, and seasonings in a bowl and form into patties. Grill in a pan with a small amount of olive oil.

Ingredients:

-1 pound ground turkey

-1/4 cup breadcrumbs

-1/4 cup finely chopped onion

-2 cloves garlic, minced

-1 egg

-1 teaspoon Worcestershire sauce

-1 teaspoon dried parsley

-1/2 teaspoon garlic powder

-1/2 teaspoon onion powder

-1/4 teaspoon salt

-1/4 teaspoon black pepper

-4 hamburger buns

Instructions:

1. In a large bowl, combine the ground turkey, breadcrumbs, onion, garlic, egg, Worcestershire sauce, parsley, garlic powder, onion powder, salt and pepper. Mix together well.

2. Form the mixture into four patties.

3. Heat a large skillet over medium-high heat. Add the patties and cook for 4-5 minutes on each side, or until the burgers are cooked through.

4. Serve the burgers on hamburger buns with desired condiments. Enjoy!

24. Green Bean Salad:

Combine cooked green beans, tomatoes, and a small amount of olive oil, garlic, and vinegar.

Ingredients:

-1 pound green beans, trimmed

-1/2 onion, finely chopped

-2 tablespoons olive oil

-1 tablespoon red wine vinegar

-1 teaspoon sugar

-1/2 teaspoon salt

-1/4 teaspoon black pepper

Method:

1. Bring a pot of salted water to a boil.

2. Add the green beans to the boiling water and cook for 5-7 minutes, until the beans are crisp-tender. Drain and set aside.

3. In a large bowl, combine the onion, olive oil, vinegar, sugar, salt, and pepper.

4. Add the green beans to the bowl and toss to combine.

5. Serve the salad immediately, or chill in the refrigerator for up to 2 days. Enjoy

25. Cauliflower Rice:

Pulse cauliflower florets in a food processor until they resemble the texture of rice. Saute in a pan with a small amount of olive oil, garlic, and onion.

Ingredients:

-1 head of cauliflower
-3 tablespoons of butter
-Salt and pepper to taste
-Optional: Garlic, onion, herbs & spices

Instructions:

1. Cut the cauliflower into small florets and discard the stem.
2. Place the florets in a food processor and pulse several times until they resemble rice-sized grains.

3. Melt the butter in a large skillet over medium heat.

4. Add the cauliflower rice to the skillet and stir to combine.

5. Cook for 5-7 minutes, stirring occasionally, until the cauliflower is cooked through.

6. Season with salt and pepper to taste.

7. For extra flavour, add garlic, onion, herbs, and spices.

8. Serve and enjoy!

26. Baked Fish:

Place a piece of wild-caught fish in a baking dish with a drizzle of olive oil, garlic, and lemon juice. Bake in the oven.

Ingredients:

-1 lb white fish fillets
-2 tablespoons olive oil
-1 teaspoon dried oregano
-1 teaspoon dried parsley
-1/2 teaspoon garlic powder
-1/2 teaspoon onion powder
-1/2 teaspoon paprika
-1/4 teaspoon cayenne pepper
-Salt and pepper, to taste

Directions:

1. Preheat oven to 375 degrees F.
2. Place fish fillets on a baking sheet lined with parchment paper.
3. In a small bowl, mix together olive oil, oregano, parsley, garlic powder, onion powder, paprika, cayenne pepper, salt and pepper.
4. Brush the mixture over both sides of the fish.
5. Bake in preheated oven for 20-25 minutes, until the fish is cooked through and flakes easily with a fork.
6. Serve with your favorite sides and enjoy!

27. Eggplant Parmesan:

Slice eggplant into rounds and top with a small amount of olive oil, garlic, and Parmesan cheese.

Ingredients:

-1 large eggplant
-1 cup of Italian breadcrumbs
-1/2 cup of grated Parmesan cheese
-1/2 cup of olive oil
-1/2 teaspoon of garlic powder
-1/2 teaspoon of dried oregano
-1/2 teaspoon of dried basil
-1/2 teaspoon of salt
-1/4 teaspoon of freshly ground black pepper
-1/2 cup of marinara sauce
-1 cup of shredded mozzarella cheese

Instructions:

1. Preheat oven to 375°F.

2. Slice the eggplant into 1/4 inch thick slices.

3. In a shallow bowl, mix the breadcrumbs, Parmesan cheese, garlic powder, oregano, basil, salt, and pepper.

4. Dip each eggplant slice into the breadcrumb mixture and press lightly to coat both sides.

5. Heat the olive oil in a large skillet over medium-high heat.

6. Fry the eggplant slices for about 3 minutes on each side, or until golden brown.

7. Place the fried eggplant slices in a single layer on a baking sheet.

8. Bake for 15 minutes.

9. Spread the marinara sauce over the eggplant slices and sprinkle with mozzarella cheese.

10. Bake for an additional 10 minutes or until the cheese is melted and bubbly.

11. Serve hot. Enjoy!

2. Lunch Recipes

Preparing lunch for diabetic and obese individuals is a crucial aspect of maintaining one's health. For these people, it's crucial to make sure that meals are balanced and include the right nutrients. For individuals who are overweight or diabetic, this article will provide suggestions for preparing balanced, healthful lunches. Meal planning, portion control, and nutrition will all be covered. Lunch meal preparation can be a fun and wholesome experience with the appropriate advice.

1. Zucchini Noodles with Turkey Meatballs:

Zucchini, Ground Turkey, Onion, Garlic, Parsley, Oregano, Salt, Pepper, Olive Oil

Ingredients:

- 2 large zucchinis
- 1 pound ground turkey
- 1/2 cup Italian-style breadcrumbs
- 1/4 cup grated Parmesan cheese
- 1 egg
- 1/2 teaspoon garlic powder
- 1/4 teaspoon onion powder
- 1/4 teaspoon salt
- 1/4 teaspoon black pepper
- 2 tablespoons olive oil
- 2 cloves garlic, minced
- 1/2 cup low-sodium chicken broth
- 1/4 cup chopped fresh parsley

Steps:

1. Preheat oven to 400 degrees Fahrenheit.

2. In a large bowl, combine the ground turkey, breadcrumbs, Parmesan cheese, egg, garlic powder, onion powder, salt, and pepper. Mix until ingredients are well combined.

3. Form the mixture into 1-inch meatballs and transfer to a baking sheet lined with parchment paper. Bake in preheated oven for 15-20 minutes, or until the meatballs are cooked through.

4. Meanwhile, use a spiralizer or mandoline to slice the zucchini into thin noodles.

5. Heat the olive oil in a large skillet over medium heat. Add the garlic and cook for 1 minute.

6. Add the zucchini noodles and chicken broth to the skillet. Cook for 3-5 minutes, stirring occasionally, until the noodles are tender.

7. Add the cooked meatballs to the skillet and stir to combine. Cook for an additional 2-3 minutes.

8. Remove the skillet from heat and stir in the chopped parsley.

9. Serve the zucchini noodles and turkey meatballs warm. Enjoy!

2. Roasted Cauliflower Rice Bowl:

Cauliflower, Onion, Garlic, Parsley, Olive Oil, Lemon Juice, Salt, Pepper

Ingredients:

-1 head of cauliflower, cut into florets

-1 tablespoon olive oil

-1/2 teaspoon smoked paprika

-1/2 teaspoon garlic powder

-1/4 teaspoon ground black pepper

-1/2 teaspoon salt

-1/4 cup grated Parmesan cheese

-1/4 cup chopped parsley

-1/4 cup toasted slivered almonds

-1/4 cup cooked quinoa

-1/4 cup cooked black beans

Instructions:

1. Preheat oven to 400 degrees F.

2. Place the cauliflower florets on a baking sheet.

3. Drizzle with olive oil and sprinkle with the smoked paprika, garlic powder, pepper, and salt.

4. Toss to coat the cauliflower evenly.

5. Roast in the oven for 20-25 minutes, stirring halfway through, until golden brown and tender.

6. Remove from the oven and transfer to a large bowl.

7. Add the Parmesan cheese, parsley, and almonds, and stir to combine.

8. Divide the roasted cauliflower among four bowls.

9. Top each bowl with the quinoa and black beans.

10. Serve and enjoy!

3. Broccoli and Quinoa Salad:

Broccoli, Quinoa, Tomatoes, Carrots, Olives, Olive Oil, Lemon Juice, Salt, Pepper

Ingredients:

-1 cup cooked quinoa

-1 head broccoli, chopped

-1/4 cup olive oil

-2 tablespoons freshly squeezed lemon juice

-2 cloves garlic, minced

-1/4 teaspoon sea salt

-freshly ground black pepper, to taste

-1/4 cup crumbled feta cheese

-1/4 cup chopped fresh parsley

Instructions:

1. Cook the quinoa according to package instructions and set aside to cool.

2. In a large bowl, combine the chopped broccoli, olive oil, lemon juice, garlic, salt, and pepper. Toss to combine.

3. Add the cooked quinoa and feta cheese to the bowl and toss to combine.

4. Sprinkle with the chopped parsley and serve. Enjoy!

4. Turkey and Sweet Potato Hash:

Turkey, Sweet Potatoes, Onion, Garlic, Parsley, Olive Oil, Salt, Pepper

Ingredients:

- 2 tablespoons olive oil
- 1 onion, diced
- 2 cloves garlic, minced
- 1 red pepper, diced
- 2 cups cooked turkey, diced
- 2 cups cooked sweet potatoes, diced
- 1 teaspoon paprika
- 1 teaspoon dried oregano
- Salt and pepper to taste

Instructions:

1. Heat the olive oil in a large skillet over medium heat.

2. Add the onion and garlic and cook until softened, about 5 minutes.

3. Add the red pepper and cook for an additional 2 minutes.

4. Add the turkey, sweet potatoes, paprika, oregano, salt, and pepper and cook for 8-10 minutes, stirring occasionally, until the vegetables are tender.

5. Serve the hash warm.

5. Turkey Lettuce Wraps:

Ground Turkey, Lettuce, Onions, Garlic, Parsley, Olive Oil, Lemon Juice, Salt, Pepper

Ingredients:

-1 pound ground turkey

-1/4 cup hoisin sauce

-1/4 cup soy sauce

-2 tablespoons sesame oil

-1 teaspoon garlic powder

-1/2 teaspoon ground ginger

-1/4 teaspoon black pepper

-1 head lettuce, leaves separated

-1/4 cup diced red onion

-1/4 cup diced carrots

-1/4 cup diced celery

-1/4 cup chopped peanuts

Instructions:

1. In a large skillet, cook the ground turkey over medium-high heat until fully cooked. Drain any excess fat.

2. In a small bowl, mix together the hoisin sauce, soy sauce, sesame oil, garlic powder, ground ginger, and black pepper.

3. Pour the sauce over the cooked turkey and reduce heat to low. Simmer for 5 minutes.

4. Remove the turkey from the heat and set aside.

5. To assemble the wraps, lay a lettuce leaf flat on a plate. Top with the turkey mixture, red onion, carrots, celery, and peanuts.

6. Roll up the wrap and enjoy!

6. Tomato and Spinach Salad:

Tomatoes, Spinach, Olive Oil, Lemon Juice, Salt, Pepper

Ingredients

- 2 tomatoes, diced
- 2 cups fresh spinach, chopped
- 1/4 cup feta cheese, crumbled
- 2 tablespoons olive oil
- 1 tablespoon balsamic vinegar
- Salt and pepper, to taste

Instructions

1. In a large bowl, combine diced tomatoes, chopped spinach, and crumbled feta cheese.
2. In a small bowl, whisk together olive oil, balsamic vinegar, salt, and pepper.
3. Pour the dressing over the salad and toss until everything is evenly coated.
4. Serve the salad immediately, or chill in the refrigerator until ready to serve. Enjoy!

7. Baked Salmon with Asparagus:

Salmon, Asparagus, Olive Oil, Lemon Juice, Salt, Pepper

Ingredients:

-1 lb salmon fillet

-1 lb asparagus

-1/4 cup olive oil

-2 cloves garlic, minced

-2 tablespoons fresh lemon juice

-1 teaspoon dried dill weed

-1/2 teaspoon salt

-1/4 teaspoon black pepper

Steps:

1. Preheat oven to 375 degrees F (190 degrees C).

2. Grease a baking dish with a little olive oil.

3. Place salmon fillet in the prepared baking dish.

4. In a small bowl, combine olive oil, garlic, lemon juice, dill weed, salt, and pepper. Stir until ingredients are well combined.

5. Pour the mixture over the salmon fillet.

6. Arrange the asparagus around the salmon fillet.

7. Bake in preheated oven for 20 minutes, or until the salmon is cooked through and the asparagus is tender.

8. Serve hot. Enjoy!

8. Zucchini Fritters:

Zucchini, Onion, Garlic, Parsley, Olive Oil, Salt, Pepper

Ingredients:

2 medium sized zucchinis

1/2 cup all-purpose flour

2 tablespoons of minced fresh parsley

1 teaspoon of baking powder

1/2 teaspoon of garlic powder

1/2 teaspoon of salt

1/4 teaspoon of ground black pepper

1 large egg, lightly beaten

1/4 cup of grated Parmesan cheese

Instructions:

1. Preheat oven to 400 degrees F. Line a baking sheet with parchment paper.

2. Grate the zucchinis using a box grater or food processor. Place the grated zucchinis in a large bowl.

3. Add the flour, parsley, baking powder, garlic powder, salt, and pepper to the zucchinis and mix until combined.

4. In a separate bowl, whisk together the egg and Parmesan cheese.

5. Pour the egg mixture into the zucchini mixture and stir until everything is well combined.

6. Take a spoonful of the mixture and form it into a patty. Place the patty on the parchment-lined baking sheet and repeat with the remaining mixture.

7. Bake the fritters for 15-20 minutes, or until golden brown and cooked through.

8. Serve warm with your favorite dipping sauce. Enjoy!

9. Egg Salad with Avocado:

Eggs, Avocado, Onion, Parsley, Olive Oil, Lemon Juice, Salt, Pepper

Ingredients:

-4 eggs

-2 tablespoons mayonnaise

-1/4 teaspoon Dijon mustard

-1/4 teaspoon garlic powder

-1/4 teaspoon onion powder

-1/4 teaspoon paprika

-1/4 teaspoon salt

-1/4 teaspoon pepper

-1 avocado, diced

-2 tablespoons diced red onion

-2 tablespoons diced celery

Method:

1. Place eggs in a medium saucepan and fill with cold water until the eggs are completely covered. Bring the water to a boil over high heat, then reduce the heat to low and simmer for 8 minutes. Remove the eggs from the heat and run cold water over them until they are cool. Peel the eggs and dice them.

2. In a medium bowl, mix together the mayonnaise, Dijon mustard, garlic powder, onion powder, paprika, salt, and pepper until combined.

3. Add the diced eggs, diced avocado, diced red onion, and diced celery to the bowl with the mayonnaise mixture and stir everything together until combined.

4. Serve the egg salad with avocado with crackers, or on a bed of lettuce. Enjoy!

10. Cucumber and Tomato Salad:

Cucumber, Tomatoes, Olive Oil, Lemon Juice, Salt, Pepper

Ingredients:

1 cucumber

2 tomatoes

1 tablespoon of chopped fresh parsley

2 tablespoons of olive oil

1 tablespoon of lemon juice

Salt and pepper to taste

Instructions:

1. Wash the cucumber and tomatoes and cut them into small cubes.

2. Put the cucumbers and tomatoes in a bowl and add the chopped parsley.

3. In a separate bowl, whisk together the olive oil, lemon juice, salt, and pepper.

4. Pour the dressing over the cucumber and tomato mixture and mix until everything is evenly coated.

5. Serve the salad chilled or at room temperature. Enjoy!

11. Grilled Chicken and Vegetables:

Chicken, Vegetables (such as peppers, zucchini, mushrooms, onions), Olive Oil, Salt, Pepper.

Ingredients:

-4 skinless, boneless chicken breasts

-1 onion, diced

-1 red bell pepper, diced

-1 yellow bell pepper, diced

-2 cloves garlic, minced

-2 tablespoons olive oil

-1 teaspoon dried oregano

-1 teaspoon dried basil

-1 teaspoon paprika

-Salt and pepper, to taste

Instructions:

1. Preheat the grill to medium-high heat.

2. In a large bowl, combine the diced onion, red and yellow bell pepper, garlic, olive oil, oregano, basil, paprika, salt and pepper. Mix until everything is evenly combined.

3. Place the chicken breasts in the bowl and toss to coat with the vegetables and seasonings.

4. Place the chicken and vegetables on the preheated grill, making sure to not overcrowd the grill. Cook for 5-7 minutes, flipping once, or until the chicken is cooked through and the vegetables are tender.

5. Remove the chicken and vegetables from the grill and serve immediately. Enjoy!

12. Quinoa Bowl with Roasted Veggies:

Quinoa, Veggies (such as peppers, zucchini, mushrooms, onions), Olive Oil, Lemon Juice, Salt, Pepper

Ingredients:

- 2 cups cooked quinoa
- 2 cups of mixed vegetables (e.g., bell peppers, zucchini, onions, mushrooms, etc.)
- 2 tablespoons olive oil
- Salt and pepper to taste
- Optional: 1/4 cup chopped fresh herbs (e.g., parsley, basil, cilantro, oregano, etc.)

Instructions:

1. Preheat the oven to 400 degrees F.
2. Spread the mixed vegetables on a baking sheet and drizzle with olive oil. Sprinkle with salt and pepper and toss to coat.
3. Roast in the oven for 20-25 minutes, or until the vegetables are tender and lightly browned.
4. Meanwhile, cook the quinoa according to package instructions.
5. When the vegetables are done, remove from the oven and let cool slightly.
6. Place the cooked quinoa in a large bowl and top with the roasted vegetables.
7. Sprinkle with chopped fresh herbs, if using.
8. Serve and enjoy!

13. Grilled Fish with Green Beans:

Fish, Green Beans, Olive Oil, Lemon Juice, Salt, Pepper

Ingredients:

-1 lb of white fish fillets (such as cod, haddock, or tilapia)

-1 tablespoon of olive oil

-1 teaspoon of garlic powder

-1/2 teaspoon of salt

-1/2 teaspoon of black pepper

-1/2 teaspoon of smoked paprika

-1 lb of green beans, trimmed

Method:

1. Preheat the grill to medium-high heat.

2. In a small bowl, mix together the olive oil, garlic powder, salt, black pepper, and smoked paprika.

3. Brush both sides of the fish fillets with the seasoning mixture.

4. Place the fish on the preheated grill and cook for 4-5 minutes per side, or until the fish flakes easily with a fork.

5. While the fish is cooking, in a medium bowl, toss the green beans with a small amount of olive oil and salt.

6. Place the green beans on the grill and cook for 3-4 minutes, or until they are tender but still crisp.

7. Serve the grilled fish and green beans warm. Enjoy

14. Turkey Burgers with Sweet Potato Fries:

Ground Turkey, Sweet Potatoes, Onion, Garlic, Parsley, Olive Oil, Salt, Pepper

Ingredients:

-Ground turkey

-Olive oil

-Onion

-Garlic

-Paprika

-Cumin

-Salt

-Pepper

-Sweet potatoes

-Buns

Step by Step Method:

1. Preheat the oven to 400 degrees F.

2. Heat 1 tablespoon of olive oil in a large skillet over medium-high heat.

3. Add the onion and garlic and cook until the onion is softened, about 5 minutes.

4. Add the ground turkey and season with paprika, cumin, salt, and pepper. Cook until the turkey is cooked through, about 10 minutes.

5. Peel and cut the sweet potatoes into fries. Place on a baking sheet, drizzle with olive oil, and season with salt and pepper. Bake for 20 minutes, flipping once halfway through.

6. Toast the buns.

7. Assemble the burgers with the turkey, onion and garlic mixture, and sweet potato fries.

15. Turkey and Spinach Lasagna:

Ground Turkey, Spinach, Onions, Garlic, Parsley, Olive Oil, Salt, Pepper

Ingredients:

- 2 tablespoons olive oil
- 1 onion, diced
- 2 cloves garlic, minced
- 1 pound ground turkey
- 1 teaspoon oregano
- 1 teaspoon basil
- 1/2 teaspoon thyme
- 1/2 teaspoon salt
- 1/4 teaspoon black pepper
- 2 cups marinara sauce
- 1 (9-ounce) package frozen chopped spinach, thawed and squeezed dry
- 1 (15-ounce) container ricotta cheese
- 2 cups shredded mozzarella cheese
- 2 large eggs
- 1/4 cup grated Parmesan cheese
- 1 (8-ounce) package lasagna noodles

Instructions:

1. Preheat oven to 350°F.

2. Heat oil in a large skillet over medium heat. Add onion and garlic and cook until softened, about 5 minutes. Add turkey and cook, breaking up with a wooden spoon, until no longer pink, about 8 minutes. Stir in oregano, basil, thyme, salt, and pepper; cook 1 minute more.

3. Spread 1/2 cup marinara sauce in the bottom of a 9x13-inch baking dish.

4. In a medium bowl, mix together spinach, ricotta, 1 cup mozzarella, eggs, and Parmesan.

5. Spread 1 cup marinara sauce over turkey in the skillet.

6. To assemble the lasagna, top the marinara sauce in the baking dish with a single layer of lasagna noodles. Spread half of the spinach mixture over the noodles. Top with half of the turkey mixture. Repeat with another layer of noodles, spinach mixture, and turkey mixture. Top with remaining noodles and marinara sauce. Sprinkle with remaining 1 cup mozzarella cheese.

7. Cover with foil and bake for 40 minutes. Uncover and bake 10 minutes more. Let cool 10 minutes before serving. Enjoy!

16. Roasted Brussels Sprouts and Sweet Potatoes:

Brussels Sprouts, Sweet Potatoes, Olive Oil, Salt, Pepper

Ingredients:

-1 pound Brussels sprouts, ends trimmed and halved

-2 medium sweet potatoes, peeled and cubed

-2 tablespoons olive oil

-1 teaspoon garlic powder

-1 teaspoon dried oregano

-1 teaspoon smoked paprika

-Salt and pepper, to taste

Step by Step Method:

1. Preheat oven to 400 degrees F (200 degrees C).

2. Line a baking sheet with parchment paper.

3. Place Brussels sprouts and sweet potatoes on the baking sheet.

4. Drizzle olive oil over the vegetables and sprinkle with garlic powder, oregano, smoked paprika, salt, and pepper.

5. Toss to combine and spread out in a single layer.

6. Roast for 25 to 30 minutes, stirring halfway through, until Brussels sprouts and sweet potatoes are tender and golden brown.

7. Serve warm. Enjoy!

17. Stuffed Peppers:

Peppers, Ground Turkey, Onions, Garlic, Parsley, Olive Oil, Salt, Pepper

Ingredients:

- 4 bell peppers
- 1/2 onion, finely chopped
- 1 pound ground beef
- 1/2 teaspoon garlic powder
- 1 teaspoon oregano
- 1/2 teaspoon paprika
- 1/2 teaspoon salt
- 1/4 teaspoon pepper
- 1 cup cooked white or brown rice
- 1 (15 ounce) can tomato sauce

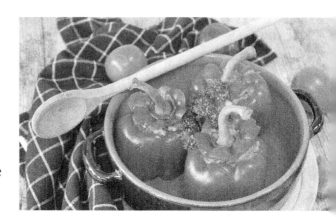

Step by Step Method:

1. Preheat oven to 350°F (175°C).
2. Cut the tops off of the bell peppers and remove the seeds and membranes.
3. Place the peppers in a large pot and cover with water. Bring to a boil and cook for 5 minutes. Drain and set aside.
4. In a large skillet over medium-high heat, cook the onion until softened.
5. Add the ground beef and cook until browned.
6. Add the garlic powder, oregano, paprika, salt and pepper.
7. Stir in the cooked rice and tomato sauce.
8. Fill each bell pepper with the beef and rice mixture.
9. Place the peppers in a baking dish and cover with foil.
10. Bake in preheated oven for 30 minutes.
11. Uncover and bake for an additional 10 minutes.
12. Serve and enjoy!

18. Baked Cod with Broccoli:

Cod, Broccoli, Olive Oil, Lemon Juice, Salt, Pepper

Ingredients:
-1.5 lbs cod fillets
-2 tablespoons olive oil
-1 teaspoon garlic powder
-1/2 teaspoon paprika
-1/4 teaspoon salt
-1/4 teaspoon black pepper
-1/4 teaspoon dried oregano
-1/4 teaspoon dried thyme
-2 cups fresh broccoli florets
-2 tablespoons freshly grated Parmesan cheese

Instructions:
1. Preheat oven to 400°F. Grease a 9x13 inch baking dish.
2. Place cod fillets in the prepared baking dish. Drizzle with olive oil and sprinkle with garlic powder, paprika, salt, pepper, oregano and thyme.
3. Arrange the broccoli florets around the cod fillets.
4. Bake in preheated oven for 15-20 minutes, or until the cod is cooked through and flaky.
5. Sprinkle with Parmesan cheese and serve.

19. Lentil Soup:

Lentils, Vegetables (such as peppers, zucchini, mushrooms, onions), Olive Oil, Salt, Pepper

Ingredients:

- 1 cup dried green lentils
- 1 large onion, diced
- 2 cloves garlic, minced
- 2 tablespoons olive oil
- 1 teaspoon dried oregano
- 4 cups vegetable broth
- 2 cups water
- 1 teaspoon ground cumin
- 1 bay leaf
- Salt and pepper to taste

Instructions:

1. In a large pot, heat the olive oil over medium heat.
2. Add the diced onion and garlic and sauté until softened, about 5 minutes.
3. Add the dried lentils, oregano, cumin, and bay leaf and stir to combine.
4. Pour in the vegetable broth and water, and bring to a boil.
5. Reduce the heat to low and simmer for 30 minutes, or until the lentils are tender.
6. Remove from heat and season with salt and pepper to taste.
7. Serve the soup hot, with your favorite toppings

20. Quinoa Stuffed Acorn Squash:

Quinoa, Acorn Squash, Onion, Garlic, Parsley, Olive Oil, Salt, Pepper

Ingredients:

- 2 medium acorn squash
- 1 cup quinoa
- 2 tablespoons olive oil
- 1 small onion, diced
- 1 red bell pepper, diced
- 2 cloves garlic, minced
- 1 teaspoon ground cumin
- 1 teaspoon dried oregano
- 1/2 teaspoon smoked paprika
- 1/4 teaspoon ground cinnamon
- 1/4 teaspoon ground black pepper
- 1/4 teaspoon sea salt
- 2 cups vegetable broth
- 2 tablespoons freshly squeezed lemon ju
- 2 tablespoons chopped fresh parsley

Instructions:

1. Preheat oven to 375°F (190°C). Line a baking sheet with parchment paper.

2. Cut the acorn squash in half and scoop out the seeds. Place the squash halves on the prepared baking sheet, cut-side up. Drizzle with 1 tablespoon of olive oil and season with a pinch of salt and pepper. Bake for 30 minutes, or until tender.

3. Meanwhile, heat remaining olive oil in a large skillet over medium heat. Add the onion and bell pepper and cook for 4-5 minutes, stirring occasionally, until softened.

4. Add the garlic, cumin, oregano, smoked paprika, cinnamon, black pepper, and salt and stir to combine.

5. Add the quinoa and broth and bring to a boil. Reduce heat to low, cover, and simmer for 15-20 minutes, or until quinoa has absorbed all the liquid.

6. Remove from heat and stir in the lemon juice and parsley.

7. Spoon the quinoa mixture into the squash halves. Bake for an additional 10 minutes, or until the tops are golden and the squash is tender.

8. Serve warm, garnished with additional parsley, if desired. Enjoy!

21. Baked Chicken with Sweet Potato:

Chicken, Sweet Potatoes, Onion, Garlic, Parsley, Olive Oil, Salt, Pepper

Ingredients:

-4 boneless, skinless chicken breasts

-1 tablespoon olive oil

-1 teaspoon garlic powder

-1 teaspoon onion powder

-1 teaspoon paprika

-1 teaspoon ground black pepper

-1/2 teaspoon salt

-2 sweet potatoes, peeled and cut into 1-inch cubes

Instructions:

1. Preheat oven to 375 degrees.
2. Place the chicken breasts in a baking dish.
3. Drizzle with olive oil, then sprinkle with garlic powder, onion powder, paprika, black pepper, and salt.
4. Toss the sweet potatoes in the baking dish, making sure they are evenly coated with the spices.
5. Bake for 25-30 minutes, or until the chicken is cooked through and the sweet potatoes are tender.
6. Serve and enjoy!

22. Turkey and Zucchini Meatballs:

Ground Turkey, Zucchini, Onion, Garlic, Parsley, Oregano, Salt, Pepper, Olive Oil

Ingredients:

-1 lb ground turkey

-1 zucchini, grated

-1/4 cup breadcrumbs

-1/4 cup grated Parmesan cheese

-1/4 cup finely chopped fresh parsley

-1 egg

-2 cloves garlic, minced

-1 tsp dried oregano

-1/2 tsp salt

-1/4 tsp black pepper

Instructions:

1. Preheat oven to 400°F (200°C). Line a baking sheet with parchment paper and set aside.

2. In a large bowl, combine ground turkey, zucchini, breadcrumbs, Parmesan cheese, parsley, egg, garlic, oregano, salt, and pepper. Mix well until all ingredients are well incorporated.

3. Scoop out 1-2 tablespoons of the turkey mixture and form into balls. Place onto the prepared baking sheet.

4. Bake in preheated oven for 20-25 minutes, or until the meatballs are cooked through and golden brown.

5. Serve warm with your favorite side dish. Enjoy!

23. Avocado and Egg Salad:

Avocado, Eggs, Onion, Parsley, Olive Oil, Lemon Juice, Salt, Pepper

Ingredients:

-2 large avocados

-4 hard-boiled eggs

-1/4 cup onion, diced

-1/4 cup celery, diced

-1/4 cup mayonnaise

-2 tablespoons fresh lemon juice

-1/2 teaspoon garlic powder

-Salt and pepper, to taste

Instructions:

1. Peel and dice the avocados and place them in a large bowl.

2. Peel and dice the hard-boiled eggs and add them to the bowl with the avocados.

3. Add the diced onion and celery to the bowl.

4. In a separate bowl, mix together the mayonnaise, lemon juice, garlic powder, salt and pepper.

5. Pour the mayonnaise mixture over the avocado and egg mixture and mix together until everything is evenly coated.

6. Serve the avocado and egg salad and enjoy!

24. Broccoli and Quinoa Bowl:

Broccoli, Quinoa, Onion, Garlic, Parsley, Olive Oil, Lemon Juice, Salt, Pepper

Ingredients:

-1 cup of quinoa

-1 cup of broccoli florets

-1/4 cup of olive oil

-Salt and pepper to taste

Steps:

1. Preheat oven to 375 degrees.

2. Wash and rinse the quinoa. Place the quinoa in a medium pot and add 2 cups of water. Bring the water to a boil and then reduce heat to low and simmer for 15 minutes.

3. In a large bowl, combine the broccoli florets, olive oil, salt and pepper. Toss to coat.

4. Spread the broccoli mixture onto a baking sheet and bake for 15 minutes.

5. Once the quinoa is done cooking, fluff it with a fork and add it to the bowl with the broccoli.

6. Serve the broccoli and quinoa bowl warm and enjoy.

25. Roasted Veggies and Brown Rice:

Veggies (such as peppers, zucchini, mushrooms, onions), Brown Rice, Olive Oil, Salt, Pepper

Ingredients:

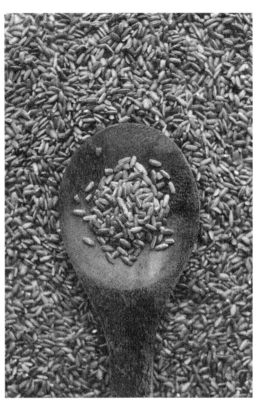

-1 cup of uncooked brown rice

-2 bell peppers (any color), diced

-1 onion, diced

-2 carrots, diced

-2 cloves garlic, minced

-1/2 teaspoon of oregano

-1/2 teaspoon of black pepper

-2 tablespoons of olive oil

-1/2 teaspoon of sea salt

Instructions:

1. Preheat oven to 400 degrees F.

2. Line a baking sheet with parchment paper and set aside.

3. In a large bowl, combine bell peppers, onion, carrots, garlic, oregano, pepper, olive oil, and sea salt. Mix until vegetables are evenly coated.

4. Spread vegetables on prepared baking sheet and roast for 20 minutes.

5. While the vegetables are roasting, cook the brown rice according to package instructions.

6. Once the vegetables are done roasting, serve over the cooked brown rice. Enjoy!

26. Baked Salmon with Asparagus:

Salmon, Asparagus, Olive Oil, Lemon Juice, Salt, Pepper

Ingredients:

• 2 salmon fillets
• 1 bunch asparagus
• 2 tablespoons olive oil
• 1 tablespoon lemon juice
• Salt and pepper
• 2 teaspoons dried herbs
(such as thyme, oregano, basil, etc.)

Steps:

1. Preheat oven to 400°F.

2. Line a baking sheet with parchment paper.

3. Place the salmon fillets on the parchment paper and season with salt and pepper.

4. Drizzle the olive oil and lemon juice over the salmon.

5. Sprinkle the dried herbs over the salmon.

6. Arrange the asparagus around the salmon and season with salt and pepper.

7. Bake for 15 minutes or until the salmon is cooked through.

8. Serve and enjoy!

27. Grilled Chicken and Veggies:

Chicken, Veggies (such as peppers, zucchini, mushrooms, onions), Olive Oil, Salt, Pepper

Ingredients:

- 2 boneless skinless chicken breasts
- 1 bell pepper, cut into strips
- 1 onion, cut into strips
- 2 tablespoons olive oil
- Salt and pepper to taste

Method:

1. Preheat the grill to medium-high heat.

2. Place the chicken breasts on a plate and season both sides with salt and pepper.

3. Place the bell pepper and onion strips on a baking sheet and toss with the olive oil.

4. Place the chicken, bell pepper, and onion strips onto the preheated grill.

5. Cook the chicken for 7-8 minutes per side, or until the internal temperature reads 165 degrees Fahrenheit.

6. Cook the bell pepper and onion strips for 5 minutes, or until they have softened and are slightly charred.

7. Serve the grilled chicken and vegetables with your favorite side dish. Enjoy

28. Lentil and Quinoa Salad:

Lentils, Quinoa, Tomatoes, Carrots, Olives, Olive Oil, Lemon Juice, Salt, Pepper
Ingredients:

- 1/2 cup green lentils
- 1/2 cup quinoa
- 2 cups water
- 1/4 cup olive oil
- 2 tablespoons lemon juice
- 2 cloves garlic, minced
- 1/2 teaspoon salt
- 1/2 teaspoon ground black pepper
- 1/2 cup diced red onion
- 1/2 cup diced celery
- 1/2 cup diced red bell pepper
- 1/4 cup chopped fresh parsley

Instructions:

1. Rinse lentils and quinoa in a fine-mesh sieve.

2. In a medium saucepan, bring the water to a boil. Add the lentils and quinoa, reduce heat to low, and simmer for 15 minutes, or until the lentils and quinoa are tender.

3. Drain any remaining water from the lentils and quinoa and transfer to a large bowl.

4. In a small bowl, whisk together the olive oil, lemon juice, garlic, salt, and pepper.

5. Pour the dressing over the lentils and quinoa and stir to combine.

6. Add the red onion, celery, red bell pepper,

29. Baked Tofu with Broccoli:

Tofu, Broccoli, Olive Oil, Salt, Pepper

Ingredients

- 1/2 block firm or extra-firm tofu, pressed
and cut into cubes
- 1/2 cup vegetable broth
- 2 tablespoons soy sauce
- 2 tablespoons sesame oil
- 2 cloves garlic, minced
- 1/4 teaspoon ground ginger
- 1/4 teaspoon red pepper flakes (optional)
- 2 cups broccoli florets
- 1/4 cup sliced almonds (optional)

Instructions

1. Preheat oven to 400 degrees Fahrenheit.
2. In a small bowl, mix together the vegetable broth, soy sauce, sesame oil, garlic, ginger, and red pepper flakes.
3. Place the cubed tofu in a 9x13 inch baking dish and pour the marinade over the tofu. Gently stir to coat the tofu in the marinade.
4. Bake the tofu for 25 minutes, stirring every 10 minutes.
5. Add the broccoli florets to the baking dish and stir to combine. Bake for an additional 15 minutes.
6. Remove the baking dish from the oven and sprinkle the almonds over the top. Serve warm.

30. Egg and Avocado Wrap:

Eggs, Avocado, Lettuce, Onion, Parsley, Olive Oil, Lemon Juice, Salt, Pepper

Ingredients:

2 eggs

1 ripe avocado

Salt and pepper

1 tablespoon olive oil

2 whole wheat wraps

Step by Step Method:

1. Crack the eggs into a bowl and whisk them together with a pinch of salt and pepper.
2. Heat the olive oil in a skillet over medium-high heat.
3. Add the eggs to the skillet and scramble until cooked, about 3 minutes.
4. Cut the avocado in half and remove the pit. Scoop out the flesh and mash with a fork.
5. Place the wraps on a clean work surface.
6. Spread the mashed avocado onto each wrap.
7. Divide the scrambled eggs evenly between the two wraps.
8. Roll up the wraps and enjoy!

3. Dinner Recipes

People who are controlling diabetes and obesity should especially refer to this chapter of meal dishes. We have assembled a selection of mouthwatering and nutritious recipes that put an emphasis on whole foods and low-calorie components since we are aware that maintaining both of these criteria may be difficult. You may enjoy tasty dinners while maintaining a healthy lifestyle thanks to the dishes' abundance of wholesome components.

1. Baked Salmon with Asparagus

Ingredients:

-4 (4-ounce) salmon fillets

-1/4 teaspoon garlic powder

-1/4 teaspoon onion powder

-1/4 teaspoon paprika

-1/4 teaspoon dried oregano

-1/4 teaspoon ground black pepper

-1/4 teaspoon sea salt

-1/4 teaspoon dried thyme

-2 tablespoons freshly squeezed lemon juice

-1 tablespoon extra-virgin olive oil

-2 tablespoons butter, melted

-1/2 pound asparagus, cut into 1-inch pieces

-2 tablespoons grated Parmesan cheese

Step by Step Method:

1. Preheat the oven to 400 degrees F.

2. Line a baking sheet with aluminum foil and lightly grease it with cooking spray.

3. In a small bowl, combine the garlic powder, onion powder, paprika, oregano, pepper, salt and thyme.

4. Place the salmon fillets on the prepared baking sheet. Sprinkle the spice mixture over the salmon and then drizzle with the lemon juice and olive oil.

5. In a separate bowl, combine the melted butter and asparagus and mix until the asparagus is coated.

6. Place the asparagus around the salmon on the baking sheet. Sprinkle the Parmesan cheese over the salmon and asparagus.

7. Bake in the preheated oven for 15 minutes, or until the salmon is cooked through and the asparagus is tender.

8. Serve the salmon and asparagus hot. Enjoy!

2. Roasted Chicken Breast with Broccoli

Ingredients:

- 4 boneless, skinless chicken breasts
- 2 tablespoons olive oil
- Salt and pepper, to taste
- 2 cups broccoli florets
- 2 tablespoons butter

Instructions:

1. Preheat oven to 400°F.
2. Place chicken breasts on a baking sheet lined with parchment paper. Drizzle with olive oil and season with salt and pepper.
3. Bake in preheated oven for 20 minutes.
4. Meanwhile, steam broccoli florets until tender.
5. Remove chicken from oven and top with butter.
6. Return to the oven and bake for an additional 10 minutes, or until chicken is cooked through.
7. Serve chicken with broccoli and enjoy!

3. Grilled Turkey and Vegetable Stir-Fry

Ingredients:

- 2 tablespoons vegetable oil
- 1 pound ground turkey
- 2 cloves garlic, minced
- 1 red bell pepper, chopped
- 1 green bell pepper, chopped
- 1 onion, chopped
- 1 carrot, shredded
- 2 tablespoons soy sauce
- 1 teaspoon ground ginger
- Salt and black pepper, to taste
- 2 tablespoons chopped fresh cilantro

Instructions:

1. Heat oil in a large skillet over medium-high heat. Add the ground turkey and cook, stirring and breaking apart with a wooden spoon, until no longer pink and cooked through, about 5 minutes.

2. Add the garlic, bell peppers, onion, carrot, soy sauce and ginger to the skillet. Season with salt and black pepper. Cook, stirring occasionally, until the vegetables are tender, about 5 minutes.

3. Reduce heat to low and stir in the cilantro. Simmer for an additional 2 minutes.

4. Serve warm. Enjoy!

4. Quinoa Salad with Roasted Vegetables

Ingredients:

-1 cup quinoa

-1 cup vegetable broth

-2 tablespoons extra-virgin olive oil

-1 zucchini, cut into 1/2-inch cubes

-1 red bell pepper, cut into 1/2-inch cubes

-1/2 teaspoon salt

-1/4 teaspoon freshly ground black pepper

-2 tablespoons fresh lemon juice

-2 tablespoons chopped fresh basil

Instructions:

1. Preheat oven to 425°F.

2. Rinse quinoa in a fine-mesh strainer, then place in a small saucepan with the vegetable broth. Bring to a boil, reduce the heat to low, cover, and simmer for 15 minutes.

3. Meanwhile, in a large bowl, combine the zucchini, bell pepper, olive oil, salt, and pepper. Toss to combine and spread out on a rimmed baking sheet. Roast in preheated oven for 20 minutes, stirring once halfway through.

4. Remove roasted vegetables from oven and set aside to cool.

5. When the quinoa is finished cooking, fluff with a fork and transfer to a large bowl.

6. Add the roasted vegetables, lemon juice, and basil and toss to combine.

7. Serve quinoa salad warm or at room temperature. Enjoy!

5. Slow Cooker Vegetable Soup

Ingredients:

- 2 tablespoons olive oil
- 1 onion, chopped
- 2 cloves garlic, minced
- 2 carrots, chopped
- 2 celery stalks, chopped
- 2 potatoes, diced
- 1 (14.5 ounce) can diced tomatoes
- 1 (15 ounce) can kidney beans, drained and rinsed
- 4 cups vegetable broth
- 1 teaspoon Italian seasoning
- 1 teaspoon dried basil
- 1 teaspoon dried oregano
- 1/2 teaspoon salt
- 1/4 teaspoon black pepper

Step by Step Method:

1. Heat the oil in a skillet over medium heat. Add the onion and garlic, and cook until the onion is translucent.

2. Transfer the onion and garlic to a slow cooker. Add the carrots, celery, potatoes, diced tomatoes, kidney beans, vegetable broth, Italian seasoning, basil, oregano, salt, and pepper. Stir to combine.

3. Cover and cook on low for 8 to 10 hours or on high for 4 to 6 hours.

4. Serve the soup warm. Enjoy!

6. Salmon and Brown Rice Bowl

Ingredients:

- 2 fillets of salmon
- 2 cups of cooked brown rice
- 2 tablespoons of olive oil
- 1 tablespoon of fresh lemon juice
- 1/2 teaspoon of garlic powder
- Salt and pepper, to taste

Instructions:

1. Preheat the oven to 400 degrees F.

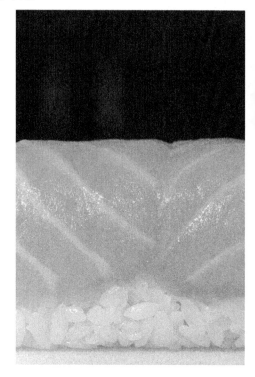

2. Place the salmon fillets on a baking sheet lined with parchment paper.

3. Drizzle the olive oil, lemon juice, garlic powder, salt, and pepper over the salmon.

4. Bake the salmon in the preheated oven for 15 minutes, or until it is cooked through.

5. Add the cooked brown rice to a bowl and top with the cooked salmon.

6. Serve the salmon and brown rice bowl with your favorite sides. Enjoy!

7. Grilled Shrimp with Zucchini and Squash

Ingredients:

-1 lb of shrimp, peeled and deveined

-2 zucchinis, cut into quarters

-2 yellow squash, cut into quarters

-2 tablespoons olive oil

-Salt and pepper

-1 teaspoon garlic powder

-1 teaspoon dried parsley

-1 teaspoon dried oregano

Instructions:

1. Preheat the grill to medium-high heat.

2. In a large bowl, combine the shrimp, zucchini, squash, olive oil, salt, pepper, garlic powder, parsley, and oregano. Toss to ensure all the ingredients are evenly coated.

3. Place the shrimp and vegetables onto the preheated grill.

4. Grill for about 5-7 minutes, flipping the shrimp and vegetables halfway through, until the shrimp is cooked through and the vegetables are tender.

5. Serve warm and enjoy!

8. Chickpea and Spinach Curry

Ingredients:

-1 tablespoon olive oil

-1 onion, chopped

-3 cloves garlic, minced

-1 teaspoon ground cumin

-1 teaspoon ground turmeric

-1 teaspoon garam masala

-1/2 teaspoon ground coriander

-1/2 teaspoon ground ginger

-1/4 teaspoon ground cardamom

-1/4 teaspoon ground cinnamon

-1/4 teaspoon cayenne pepper

-1 (14.5 ounce) can diced tomatoes

-2 cups vegetable broth

-1 (15 ounce) can chickpeas, drained and rinsed

-1 (10 ounce) package frozen chopped spinach, thawed and drained

-Salt and pepper to taste

Instructions:

1. Heat oil in a large pot over medium-high heat.

2. Add onion and garlic and cook until softened, about 5 minutes.

3. Add cumin, turmeric, garam masala, coriander, ginger, cardamom, cinnamon and cayenne pepper and cook for 1 minute.

4. Add diced tomatoes and vegetable broth and bring to a boil.

5. Reduce heat and simmer for 10 minutes.

6. Add chickpeas and spinach and cook for 5 minutes.

7. Season with salt and pepper to taste.

8. Serve hot with cooked rice or naan. Enjoy!

9. Greek Salad with Feta and Olives

Ingredients:

- 4 cups of Romaine lettuce, chopped
- 1/2 cup of diced red onion
- 1/2 cup of diced cucumber
- 1/2 cup of diced tomatoes
- 1/4 cup of pitted kalamata olives
- 1/4 cup of crumbled feta cheese
- 2 tablespoons of extra-virgin olive oil
- 2 tablespoons of fresh lemon juice
- 1 teaspoon of dried oregano
- Salt and pepper to taste

Instructions:

1. In a large bowl, combine the chopped Romaine lettuce, red onion, cucumber, tomatoes and kalamata olives.

2. In a small bowl, whisk together the olive oil, lemon juice, oregano, salt, and pepper.

3. Pour the dressing over the salad and toss to combine.

4. Sprinkle the crumbled feta cheese over the salad and serve.

10. Lentil and Kale Stew

Ingredients:

-1 tablespoon olive oil

-1 onion, finely chopped

-2 carrots, diced

-2 cloves garlic, minced

-1 teaspoon ground cumin

-1 teaspoon smoked paprika

-1/2 teaspoon dried oregano

-1/4 teaspoon ground coriander

-1/4 teaspoon ground cinnamon

-1/2 teaspoon sea salt

-1 cup dried green lentils

-4 cups vegetable broth

-2 cups chopped kale leaves

-1/4 cup fresh parsley, chopped

Instructions:

1. Heat the olive oil in a large pot over medium heat. Add the onion and carrots and cook for 5 minutes, stirring occasionally.

2. Add the garlic and spices and cook for 1 minute, stirring constantly.

3. Add the lentils, vegetable broth and 2 cups of water. Bring to a boil, then reduce the heat to low and simmer for 25 minutes, stirring occasionally.

4. Add the kale and parsley, and cook for 5 minutes more.

5. Serve and enjoy!

11. Grilled Vegetable and Tofu Kabobs

Ingredients:

-1 package extra-firm tofu

-1 red pepper

-1 zucchini

-1 red onion

-1 bell pepper

-1 tablespoon extra-virgin olive oil

-1 teaspoon garlic powder

-1 teaspoon paprika

-1 teaspoon dried oregano

-1 teaspoon dried basil

-Salt and black pepper, to taste

-1/4 cup balsamic vinegar

Instructions:

1. Preheat the grill to medium-high heat.

2. Cut the tofu into 1-inch cubes and place in a medium bowl.

3. Cut the red pepper, zucchini, red onion, and bell pepper into 1-inch cubes and add to the bowl with the tofu.

4. Drizzle the vegetables and tofu with the olive oil and season with garlic powder, paprika, oregano, basil, salt, and pepper. Gently toss to coat.

5. Thread the vegetables and tofu onto skewers, alternating the types of vegetables.

6. Place the skewers on the preheated grill and cook for 10-15 minutes, turning occasionally, until the vegetables are tender and the tofu is golden brown.

7. Remove the skewers from the grill and drizzle with balsamic vinegar. Serve hot.

12. Turkey and Quinoa Stuffed Peppers

Ingredients:

- 4 bell peppers
- 1 tablespoon olive oil
- 1 pound ground turkey
- 1 teaspoon garlic powder
- 1 teaspoon paprika
- 1/2 teaspoon salt
- 1/4 teaspoon black pepper
- 1/4 teaspoon cumin
- 1/4 teaspoon dried oregano
- 1/4 teaspoon onion powder
- 1/4 teaspoon chili powder
- 1 cup cooked quinoa
- 1/2 cup diced red onion
- 1/2 cup diced bell pepper
- 1/4 cup chopped fresh parsley
- 1/4 cup crumbled feta cheese

Instructions:

1. Preheat oven to 375°F.

2. Cut the tops off the bell peppers and remove the seeds. Place the peppers in a baking dish.

3. Heat the olive oil in a large skillet over medium-high heat. Add the ground turkey and cook, breaking it up with a spoon, until it is no longer pink, about 5 minutes.

4. Add the garlic powder, paprika, salt, pepper, cumin, oregano, onion powder, and chili powder to the turkey. Cook, stirring, for 1 minute.

5. Stir in the cooked quinoa, red onion, bell pepper, and parsley. Cook, stirring, for 3 minutes.

6. Remove the skillet from the heat and stir in the feta cheese.

7. Spoon the turkey and quinoa mixture into the bell peppers.

8. Bake in the preheated oven for 25 minutes, or until the peppers are tender. Serve warm.

13. Roasted Vegetable and Barley Bowl

Ingredients:

- 2 cups cooked barley
- 1 sweet potato, cut into 1 inch pieces
- 1 red onion, cut into wedges
- 2 tablespoons olive oil
- 2 cups broccoli florets
- 1 cup cooked chickpeas
- 1 teaspoon garlic powder
- 2 tablespoons freshly squeezed lemon juice
- 2 tablespoons chopped fresh parsley
- Salt and pepper to taste

Instructions:

1. Preheat the oven to 375 degrees F (190 degrees C).

2. Spread the sweet potato, red onion, and broccoli on a baking sheet. Drizzle with olive oil and sprinkle with garlic powder and salt.

3. Roast in the preheated oven for 25 minutes, stirring occasionally, until vegetables are tender.

4. Meanwhile, in a medium bowl, combine the cooked barley, chickpeas, lemon juice, and parsley.

5. Once the vegetables are roasted, add them to the bowl and mix everything together.

6. Taste and adjust seasonings, if needed.

7. Serve warm or at room temperature. Enjoy

14. Baked Tilapia with Tomatoes and Herbs

Ingredients:

- 4 (6-ounce) tilapia fillets
- 1 teaspoon olive oil
- 2 garlic cloves, minced
- 1/4 teaspoon salt
- 1/4 teaspoon freshly ground black pepper
- 1/4 cup dry white wine
- 2 tablespoons fresh lemon juice
- 2 tablespoons chopped fresh parsley
- 2 teaspoons chopped fresh oregano
- 2 tablespoons chopped fresh basil
- 1/4 cup diced tomatoes
- 2 tablespoons grated Parmesan cheese

Steps:

1. Preheat oven to 350 degrees F (175 degrees C).

2. Place tilapia fillets in a 9x13 inch baking dish. Drizzle with olive oil, and season with garlic, salt, and pepper.

3. Pour white wine, lemon juice, parsley, oregano, and basil over the fillets. Top with tomatoes and Parmesan cheese.

4. Bake for 20 minutes in the preheated oven, or until fish flakes easily with a fork. Serve hot.

15. Grilled Vegetable and Hummus Wraps

Ingredients:

-Tortillas

-Cucumber, sliced

-Tomato, sliced

-Red onion, sliced

-Bell pepper, sliced

-Mushrooms, sliced

-Olive oil

-Salt and pepper

-Hummus

Steps:

1. Preheat a grill to medium heat.

2. Place the cucumber, tomato, red onion, bell pepper, and mushrooms on a sheet pan. Drizzle with olive oil and season with salt and pepper.

3. Grill the vegetables until tender, about 5 minutes, flipping halfway through.

4. Heat the tortillas on the grill until lightly charred, about 1 minute per side.

5. Spread a layer of hummus on each tortilla.

6. Top with the grilled vegetables.

7. Roll up the tortillas and enjoy!

16. Spaghetti Squash with Turkey Meatballs

Ingredients:

-1 spaghetti squash

-1 lb ground turkey

-1/4 cup grated Parmesan cheese

-1/4 cup Italian bread crumbs

-1/4 cup finely chopped onion

-1 egg

-1 tsp garlic powder

-1/2 tsp dried oregano

-1/2 tsp dried basil

-3/4 tsp salt

-1/4 tsp black pepper

-2 cups marinara sauce

-1/4 cup chopped fresh parsley (optional)

Method:

1. Preheat oven to 375 degrees F.

2. Cut the spaghetti squash in half lengthwise, scoop out the seeds and place cut side down on a baking sheet lined with parchment paper. Roast in preheated oven for 30 minutes.

3. Meanwhile, combine the ground turkey, Parmesan cheese, bread crumbs, onion, egg, garlic powder, oregano, basil, salt and pepper in a large bowl. Mix well to combine. Form into 1-inch meatballs.

4. Heat a large skillet over medium heat. Add the meatballs and cook until browned and cooked through, about 8-10 minutes.

5. Remove the spaghetti squash from the oven. Using a fork, scrape the strands of squash into a large bowl.

6. Add the marinara sauce and meatballs to the spaghetti squash and mix to combine.

7. Transfer the spaghetti squash and meatball mixture to the baking sheet. Bake in preheated oven for 15-20 minutes.

8. Sprinkle with chopped fresh parsley, if desired. Serve warm. Enjoy!

17. Stuffed Mushroom Caps

Ingredients:

-12 large mushrooms

-1/2 cup of grated Parmesan cheese

-1/4 cup of chopped fresh parsley

-1/4 cup of diced red onion

-2 cloves of garlic, minced

-1/4 cup of panko bread crumbs

-2 tablespoons of olive oil

-Salt and pepper to taste

Instructions:

1. Preheat oven to 375 degrees.

2. Clean mushrooms and remove stems. Place the mushroom caps on a foil-lined baking sheet and set aside.

3. In a medium bowl, mix together Parmesan cheese, parsley, red onion, garlic, panko bread crumbs, olive oil, salt, and pepper.

4. Spoon the mixture into the mushroom caps.

5. Bake in preheated oven for 20-25 minutes, or until the cheese is melted and the mushrooms are tender.

6. Serve warm. Enjoy!

18. Grilled Salmon and Vegetable Kabobs

Ingredients:

• 1 pound salmon fillet, cut into 1-inch cubes

• 1 red bell pepper, cut into 1-inch cubes

• 1 yellow bell pepper, cut into 1-inch cubes

• 1 zucchini, cut into 1/2-inch-thick slices

• 1 red onion, cut into 1-inch cubes

• 2 tablespoons olive oil

• 2 tablespoons Italian seasoning

• 1 teaspoon garlic powder

• Salt and freshly ground black pepper, to taste

• 6 wooden skewers, soaked in water for 30 minutes

Instructions:

1. Preheat the grill to medium-high heat.

2. In a large bowl, combine the salmon, bell peppers, zucchini, red onion, olive oil, Italian seasoning, garlic powder, salt, and pepper. Toss until everything is evenly coated.

3. Thread the salmon and vegetables onto the skewers.

4. Grill the kabobs for 8-10 minutes, turning every few minutes until the salmon is cooked through and the vegetables are lightly charred.

5. Serve the kabobs with your favorite sides and enjoy!

19. Zucchini Noodles with Pesto

Ingredients:

- 2 zucchinis
- 2 tablespoons of pesto
- Salt
- Pepper
- Olive oil

Steps:

1. Wash and dry the zucchinis.

2. Use a spiralizer or vegetable peeler to create zucchini noodles.

3. Heat olive oil in a large skillet over medium heat.

4. Add the zucchini noodles and cook for about 5 minutes, stirring occasionally.

5. Season with salt and pepper to taste.

6. Add the pesto and stir to combine.

7. Cook for another minute or two, until the noodles are cooked to your desired consistency.

8. Serve warm and enjoy!

20. Baked Sweet Potatoes with Greek Yogurt and Berries

Ingredients:

- 2 large sweet potatoes
- 2 tablespoons olive oil
- 2 tablespoons honey
- 2 teaspoons ground cinnamon
- 1/2 teaspoon ground nutmeg
- 1/2 teaspoon ground ginger
- 1/4 teaspoon salt
- 1/2 cup Greek yogurt
- 1/2 cup fresh or frozen berries

Instructions:

1. Preheat oven to 400 degrees F (200 degrees C).

2. Line a baking sheet with parchment paper.

3. Wash and dry sweet potatoes, then poke several holes in each with a fork.

4. Place sweet potatoes on prepared baking sheet and rub with olive oil.

5. Bake for 45-60 minutes, or until potatoes are tender when pierced with a fork.

6. In a small bowl, mix together honey, cinnamon, nutmeg, ginger and salt.

7. Once sweet potatoes are done baking, remove from oven and brush with honey-spice mixture.

8. Return to oven and bake for an additional 5-10 minutes.

9. Remove from oven and allow to cool slightly.

10. Slice sweet potatoes in half and top with Greek yogurt and berries. Enjoy!

4. Snack Recipes

Obese and diabetic people may find it difficult to snack and eat in between meals. However, it is feasible to maintain a healthy weight, support blood sugar balance, and still enjoy great snacks with mindful eating and the correct snacks. This article will provide advice on selecting healthy snacks and between-meal foods for diabetics and obese individuals so they may still enjoy their favorite foods without jeopardizing their health.

1. Celery and Hummus:

Ingredients: Celery, hummus, lemon juice, olive oil, pepper

Preparation:

1. Chop the celery into bite-sized pieces.

2. In a bowl, mix together the hummus, lemon juice, and olive oil.

3. Dip the celery pieces into the hummus mixture and season with pepper.

2. Baked Kale Chips:

Ingredients: Kale leaves, olive oil, salt

Preparation:

1. Preheat oven to 350°F.

2. Tear the kale leaves into bite-sized pieces.

3. Place the kale pieces on a baking sheet and coat with olive oil.

4. Sprinkle with salt and bake for 12-15 minutes.

3. Greek Yogurt Parfait:

Ingredients: Greek yogurt, fresh fruit, nuts, honey

Preparation:

1. Layer the yogurt, fruit, and nuts in a bowl.

2. Drizzle with honey.

3. Enjoy!

4. Smoothie Bowl:

Ingredients: Frozen fruit, Greek yogurt, almond milk, honey

Preparation:

1. Place the frozen fruit in a blender.

2. Add the yogurt and almond milk.

3. Blend until smooth.

4. Pour into a bowl and top with honey.

5. Bean Burrito:

Ingredients: Refried beans, whole-wheat tortilla, salsa, shredded cheese

Preparation:

1. Heat the refried beans in a skillet over medium heat.

2. Spread the beans onto a whole-wheat tortilla.

3. Top with salsa and cheese.

4. Roll the burrito and enjoy!

6. Avocado Toast:

Ingredients: Whole-wheat bread, avocado, lemon juice, salt

Preparation:

1. Toast the bread.

2. Mash the avocado with a fork.

3. Spread the mashed avocado on the toast.

4. Drizzle with lemon juice and sprinkle with salt.

7. Quinoa Bowl:

Ingredients: Quinoa, vegetables, olive oil, spices

Preparation:

1. Cook the quinoa according to package instructions.

2. Sauté the vegetables in a skillet with olive oil and desired spices.

3. Combine the quinoa and vegetables in a bowl and enjoy.

8. Apple Slices with Peanut Butter:

Ingredients: Apple, peanut butter

Preparation:

1. Slice the apple into thin slices.

2. Spread the peanut butter onto the apple slices.

3. Enjoy!

9. Zucchini Fries:

Ingredients: Zucchini, olive oil, parmesan cheese, breadcrumbs

Preparation:

1. Preheat oven to 400°F.

2. Slice the zucchini into fry shapes.

3. Toss the zucchini in olive oil, parmesan cheese, and breadcrumbs.

4. Place on a baking sheet and bake for 15-20 minutes.

10. Overnight Oats:

Ingredients: Oats, almond milk, chia seeds, honey

Preparation:

1. Combine the oats, almond milk, chia seeds, and honey in a bowl and mix.

2. Place the bowl in the refrigerator overnight.

3. Enjoy cold in the morning.

11. Cucumber Tomato Salad:

Ingredients: Cucumbers, tomatoes, olive oil, balsamic vinegar, salt

Preparation:

1. Dice the cucumbers and tomatoes.

2. Place the vegetables in a bowl and toss with olive oil, balsamic vinegar, and salt.

3. Enjoy!

12. Baked Sweet Potato Fries:

Ingredients: Sweet potatoes, olive oil, spices

Preparation:

1. Preheat oven to 400°F.

2. Slice the sweet potatoes into fry shapes.

3. Toss the sweet potatoes with olive oil and desired spices.

4. Place on a baking sheet and bake for 15-20 minutes.

13. Chocolate Banana Bites:

Ingredients: Banana, dark chocolate chips

Preparation:

1. Slice the banana into bite-sized pieces.

2. Place the dark chocolate chips in a bowl and melt in the microwave.

3. Dip the banana pieces in the melted chocolate.

4. Place the banana pieces on a parchment paper-lined baking sheet and freeze for at least 1 hour.

14. Chickpea Salad:

Ingredients: Chickpeas, vegetables, olive oil, lemon juice, salt

Preparation:

1. Drain and rinse the chickpeas.

2. Chop the vegetables into bite-sized pieces.

3. In a bowl, mix together the chickpeas, vegetables, olive oil, lemon juice, and salt.

4. Enjoy!

15. Edamame:

Ingredients: Edamame, salt

Preparation:

1. Bring a pot of water to a boil.

2. Add the edamame to the boiling water and cook for 3-5 minutes.

3. Drain the edamame and season with salt.

4. Enjoy!

16. Popcorn:

Ingredients: Popcorn kernels, butter, salt

Preparation:

1. Heat a pot over medium heat.

2. Add the popcorn kernels, butter, and a pinch of salt.

3. Cover the pot and shake until the popcorn is popped.

4. Enjoy!

17. Carrot Sticks and Hummus:

Ingredients: Carrots, hummus, lemon juice, olive oil, pepper

Preparation:

1. Wash and cut the carrots into sticks.

2. In a bowl, mix together the hummus, lemon juice, and olive oil.

3. Dip the carrot sticks into the hummus mixture and season with pepper.

18. Fruit Salad:

Ingredients: Fresh fruit of your choice

Preparation:

1. Wash and chop the fruit into bite-sized pieces.

2. Place the fruit in a bowl and mix together.

3. Enjoy!

19. Trail Mix:

Ingredients: Nuts, dried fruit, dark chocolate chips

Preparation:

1. Place the nuts, dried fruit, and dark chocolate chips in a bowl and mix together.

2. Enjoy!

20. Egg Salad:

Ingredients: Eggs, mayonnaise, mustard, celery, salt

Preparation:

1. Boil the eggs for 8-10 minutes.

2. Peel and mash the eggs.

3. Mix together the mashed eggs, mayonnaise, mustard, celery

5. VEGETABLE OPTIONS

Because they are natural and have lower fat and sugar contents, vegetables may also be a fantastic alternative for meals for individuals who are obese or diabetic. Here are 20 excellent ideas for diabetic and obese people's vegetable meal preparations.

1. Lentil and Kale Soup:

Ingredients – Lentils, Kale, Onion, Garlic, Olive oil, Vegetable broth.

Method - Soak lentils overnight and boil them in a pot. Sautee onion and garlic in olive oil until golden and add in kale to cook. Add vegetable broth and lentils and simmer for 15-20 minutes.

2. Broccoli and Mushroom Stir-Fry:

Ingredients – Broccoli, Mushrooms, Onion, Garlic, Olive oil, Low-sodium soy sauce.

Method - Heat olive oil in a wok and add in onion and garlic. Add mushrooms and broccoli and sauté until cooked. Add in low-sodium soy sauce and stir-fry for a few minutes.

3. Cauliflower Curry:

Ingredients – Cauliflower, Onion, Garlic, Curry powder, Coconut milk, Olive oil.

Method - Heat olive oil in a pan and add in onion and garlic. Add cauliflower and curry powder and sauté for a few minutes. Pour in coconut milk and bring to a simmer. Cook for 10-15 minutes until the cauliflower is cooked.

4. Zucchini and Tomato Bake:

Ingredients – Zucchini, Tomatoes, Onion, Garlic, Olive oil, Herbs.

Method - Preheat oven to 375 degrees. Slice zucchini and tomatoes and place in a greased baking dish. Sautee onion and garlic in olive oil and spread over the vegetables. Top with herbs and bake for 25-30 minutes.

5. Eggplant and Spinach Salad:

Ingredients – Eggplant, Spinach, Onion, Garlic, Olive oil, Lemon juice.

Method - Slice eggplant and sauté in olive oil until golden. Add onion and garlic and cook for a few minutes. Add spinach and cook until wilted. Drizzle with lemon juice and season with salt and pepper.

6. Roasted Cabbage:

Ingredients – Cabbage, Olive oil, Herbs.

Method - Preheat oven to 375 degrees. Cut cabbage into wedges and place on a baking sheet lined with parchment paper. Drizzle with olive oil and sprinkle with herbs. Bake for 25-30 minutes until golden and crispy.

7. Lentil and Carrot Stew:

Ingredients – Lentils, Carrots, Onion, Garlic, Olive oil, Vegetable broth.

Method - Heat olive oil in a pot and add in onion and garlic. Add carrots and sauté for a few minutes. Add lentils and vegetable broth and bring to a boil. Simmer for 15-20 minutes until the lentils are cooked.

8. Roasted Sweet Potato and Asparagus:

Ingredients – Sweet potato, Asparagus, Olive oil, Herbs.

Method - Preheat oven to 375 degrees. Peel and cube sweet potato and place on a baking sheet lined with parchment paper. Drizzle with olive oil and sprinkle with herbs. Add asparagus and bake for 25-30 minutes until golden and crispy.

9. Quinoa and Vegetable Bowl:

Ingredients – Quinoa, Vegetables (e.g. carrots, broccoli, mushrooms), Olive oil, Herbs.

Method - Cook quinoa according to package instructions. Sauté vegetables in olive oil until cooked. Mix together quinoa and vegetables and season with herbs.

10. Vegetable Lasagna:

Ingredients – Lasagna sheets, Tomato sauce, Vegetables (e.g. zucchini, mushrooms, spinach), Ricotta cheese, Mozzarella cheese.

Method - Preheat oven to 375 degrees. Spread a layer of tomato sauce in a greased baking dish. Layer lasagna sheets, vegetables, ricotta cheese and mozzarella cheese. Repeat layers and top with mozzarella cheese. Bake for 25-30 minutes until golden and bubbly.

11. Chickpea Curry:

Ingredients – Chickpeas, Onion, Garlic, Curry powder, Coconut milk, Olive oil.

Method - Heat olive oil in a pan and add in onion and garlic. Add curry powder and sauté for a few minutes. Add chickpeas and coconut milk and bring to a simmer. Cook for 10-15 minutes until the chickpeas are cooked.

12. Roasted Brussels Sprouts:

Ingredients – Brussels sprouts, Olive oil, Herbs.

Method - Preheat oven to 375 degrees. Halve Brussels sprouts and place on a baking sheet lined with parchment paper. Drizzle with olive oil and sprinkle with herbs. Bake for 25-30 minutes until golden and crispy.

13. Broccoli and Cauliflower Salad:

Ingredients – Broccoli, Cauliflower, Onion, Garlic, Olive oil, Lemon juice.

Method - Chop broccoli and cauliflower and place in a bowl. Sautee onion and garlic in olive oil and add to the bowl. Dress with lemon juice and season with salt and pepper.

14. Ratatouille:

Ingredients – Eggplant, Zucchini, Tomatoes, Onion, Garlic, Olive oil, Herbs.

Method - Heat olive oil in a pan and add in onion and garlic. Add eggplant, zucchini and tomatoes and cook for a few minutes. Add herbs and season with salt and pepper.

15. Butternut Squash Soup:

Ingredients – Butternut squash, Onion, Garlic, Olive oil, Vegetable broth.
Method - Peel and cube butternut squash and place in a pot. Sautee onion and garlic in olive oil and add to the pot. Pour in vegetable broth and bring to a boil. Simmer for 15 minutes until the squash is cooked.

16. Stuffed Peppers:

Ingredients – Peppers, Quinoa, Vegetables (e.g. carrots, mushrooms, spinach), Ricotta cheese, Herbs.
Method - Preheat oven to 375 degrees. Cut the tops off the peppers and remove the seeds. Cook quinoa according to package instructions. Mix together quinoa, vegetables, ricotta cheese and herbs. Stuff the peppers with the filling and bake for 25-30 minutes until golden.

17. Lentil and Spinach Salad:

Ingredients – Lentils, Spinach, Onion, Garlic, Olive oil, Lemon juice.

Method - Cook lentils according to package instructions. Sautee onion and garlic in olive oil and add to the lentils. Add spinach and cook until wilted. Dress with lemon juice and season with salt and pepper.

18. Baked Eggplant Parmesan:

Ingredients – Eggplant, Tomato sauce, Mozzarella cheese, Parmesan cheese.

Method - Preheat oven to 375 degrees. Slice eggplant and place in a greased baking dish. Top with tomato sauce and mozzarella cheese. Sprinkle with parmesan cheese and bake for 25-30 minutes until golden and bubbly.

19. Roasted Vegetable Bowl:

Ingredients – Vegetables (e.g. carrots, broccoli, cauliflower), Olive oil, Herbs.
Method - Preheat oven to 375 degrees. Peel and cube vegetables and place on a baking sheet lined with parchment paper. Drizzle with olive oil and sprinkle with herbs. Bake for 25-30 minutes until golden and crispy.

20. Cabbage and Carrot Slaw:

Ingredients – Cabbage, Carrots, Onion, Garlic, Olive oil, Lemon juice.
Method - Shred cabbage and carrots and place in a bowl. Sautee onion and garlic in olive oil and add to the bowl. Dress with lemon juice and season with salt and pepper.

C. Tips for Eating Healthy

Here are some recommendations for eating well.

1. Opt for nutrient-rich foods: Choose foods like fruits, vegetables, whole grains, lean meats, and healthy fats that are high in nutrients and low in calories.

Limit or avoid sugary drinks, sweet desserts, and other meals with added sugars.
2. Reduce added sugars.

3. Manage portion sizes: To assist you manage your portion sizes, use smaller plates, bowls, and glasses.

4. Increase fiber intake: Eat more whole grains, fruits, vegetables, nuts, and other high-fiber foods.

5. Use mindful eating to help you only eat when you are actually hungry. Pay attention to your body's hunger and fullness signals.

6. Drink extra water: Water keeps you hydrated and helps you feel full throughout the day.

7. Limit your consumption of processed foods, such as frozen meals, packaged snacks, and fast food, and avoid them altogether.

8. Regular exercise may aid in weight management and general health improvement.

9. Get adequate sleep. Sleeping sufficiently each night can help you control your blood sugar levels and maintain a high level of energy.

11. Keep an eye on your blood sugar levels: Check your blood sugar levels often to make sure they remain within a safe range.

Meal Planning and Shopping Tips

Below are Meal planning and Shopping Tips for A Low Sugar Diet.

How to schedule a week's worth of low-sugar meals

1. Choose the number of meals you wish to schedule for the week. Take into account the amount of meals you will need to prepare and the number of people you are preparing for. For instance, if you are organizing a family of four, you may schedule three meals and two snacks per day.

2. Compile a list of every item you'll need for the meals you want to prepare. You may construct a list of all the things you'll need to purchase by searching for recipes online. Include everything you need, including any staples you may already have in your cupboard, such wheat, oil, and spices.

3. Create a grocery list when you have your list of ingredients, then go shopping. Before you depart, be sure to check your pantry to make sure you don't purchase something you already own.

4. After you return from the supermarket, look up the expiry dates of everything you bought and develop a plan for the meals you'll eat that week. Think of the number of meals you'll need and the days you'll be preparing them.

5. Create a cooking schedule after you have a plan for the week. Schedule the times you will be cooking, cleaning, and preparing meals. You can remain organized and on schedule by doing this.

6. Lastly, remember to schedule time for leftovers. Plan for more things if you have dishes that can be reheated or excess components you can use for another meal.

Meal prep ideas for busy weeks

1. Make enormous amounts of meals the weekend before for easy reheating all week. Some examples are chili, casseroles, soup, spaghetti sauce, and burritos.

2. Slow-cooker meals: Prepare the ingredients in the morning, and dinner will be ready when you get home.

3. Sheet pan dinners: Before roasting on a single sheet pan, all the ingredients should be prepped and diced.

4. Stir-fry: Before serving vegetables and meats with quinoa or rice, stir-fry them for a short period of time.

5. Prepare a lot of sandwiches or wraps that you may pack for lunch all week.

6. Prepare meals in a single pot or skillet, such as a straightforward quiche or a frittata loaded with veggies.

7. Prepare food ahead of time and freeze it for quick and easy meals. Lasagna, enchiladas, and soup are a few examples.

8. Make something new out of leftovers from earlier in the week, such a soup or casserole, for Leftover Night.

9. Prepare vegetables in advance: Preparing vegetables in advance during the weekend will streamline midweek dinner preparation.

10. Prepare chopped greens and other veggies in advance in the refrigerator for quick salads.

Exercise Suggestions For Obese People

1) Jumping Jacks: This workout is excellent for burning fat. Start the exercise by placing your hands at your sides and your feet together. Then leap up, extend your legs wide, and raise your arms over your head. Restart by leaping back to the starting location. Perform three sets of 10–12 reps.

2) Running: Running is an excellent fat-burning workout. Start by warming up by strolling for five minutes. Start running after that for 20 to 30 minutes at a moderate pace. By switching between a jog and a sprint every few minutes, you may also include sprints in your run.

3) Burpees: Burpees are a great fat-burning activity. To complete the workout, begin standing up straight before bending over and doing a push-up. leap up into the air and then leap your feet back up to your hands. Restart in the original location after landing. Perform three sets of 10–12 reps.

4) Squats: Squats are an excellent fat-burning activity. Starting in a standing stance with your feet shoulder-width apart, do the exercise. After that, squat as if you were sitting on a chair, and then rise back to your starting posture. Perform three sets of 10–12 reps.

5) Mountain Climbers: Climbing mountains is an excellent fat-burning workout. Start in the push-up posture to do the workout. Bring one knee to your chest, then lower it back down. Repeat with the other leg. Perform three sets of 10–12 reps.

Conclusion

This cookbook has been created to provide tasty and wholesome meals for diabetic and obese people. It includes dishes that are high in dietary fiber, vitamins, and minerals yet low in sugar, saturated fat, and salt. The recipes are intended to make it easier for individuals with diabetes and obesity to eat well without endangering their health. Additionally, the meal plans included in the cookbook are customized to meet the requirements of each individual.

Overall, anybody trying to improve their lifestyle for the better should check out this cookbook. Individuals may enjoy delectable, nutrient-dense meals that are catered to their particular requirements with the aid of this cookbook. People may work toward attaining their health objectives and leading better lives by following the recipes and meal plans offered.

END

Printed in Great Britain
by Amazon

43705057R00079